GOD'S STRESS MANAGEMENT PLAN

Ten Biblical Principles for Avoiding, Reducing or Better Managing Stress

Dr. Helen A. Mendes

Foreword by:
Bishop Charles E. Blake
Senior Pastor, West Angeles Church of God in Christ
Los Angeles, California

God's Stress Management Plan
By Dr. Helen A. Mendes

Copyright © 2004 by Dr. Helen A. Mendes

Published by:
Vicstone Publishing Company
3660 Wilshire Blvd., Suite 907
Los Angeles, CA 90010
E-Mail: vicstone.publishing@verizon.net

Printed in the United States of America
10 9 8 7 6 5 4 3 2 1

ISBN: 0-9744482-0-6
Library of Congress Control Number: 2003113905

Source of Scriptures

Unless other wise indicated, all scripture quotations are taken from the *King James Version* of the *Bible*.

Scripture Quotations marked NKJV are taken from the *New King James Version* of the *Bible*. Copyright 1979, 1980 by Thomas Nelson, Inc. Used by permission.

Scripture quotations marked NIV are taken from *The Holy Bible, New International Version*® NIV® Copyright 1973, 1978, 1984 by International Bible Society. Used by permission of Zondervan Publishing House. All rights reserved.

Scripture quotations marked RSV are taken from the *Revised Standard Version* of the *Bible*. Copyright by Augsburg Fortress. All rights reserved.

Scripture quotations marked LBV are taken from *The Living Bible Version* of the *Bible*. Copyright 1996 by Tyndale House Publishers. All rights reserved.

*This book is dedicated to my
beloved husband and best friend,
Gregory R. Love.
His love, prodding, spiritual insight,
and computer skills have been
invaluable to me.*

CHRISTIAN VOICES

"Here is the answer for those who think they may be too stressed to feel blessed. Easy to read and digest, Dr. Mendes' principles provide a practical, empowering prescription for people of faith to effectively manage the stress that affects all of us in these challenging times."

— Pastor James J. Lobdell, Senior Pastor
Holy Trinity Evangelical Lutheran Church, Inglewood, CA

"An excellent, practical and useful book on stress management. Well written with clarity and balance. Sound biblically based solutions to some of life's most difficult struggles and stressors. A must for everyone who needs to integrate their faith into the daily rigors of life."

— Dr. Mary M. Simms, Executive Director
Family Outreach Counseling Services, Long Beach, CA

"...provides practical and specific interventions based on biblical principles to reduce your stress. What life changing news this is if practiced on a daily basis!"

— Amelia C. Roberts, Ph.D., Associate Professor, School of Social
Work, University of North Carolina, Chapel Hill, NC

"This is a great book on stress — it reveals in a clear, useable format how to implement Paul's words in Philippians 4:6: *"Be careful for nothing; but in everything by prayer and supplication with thanksgiving let your request be made known unto God."*

— Pastor Vanessa Dantzler, Senior Pastor
Apostolic Faith Home Assembly, Los Angeles, CA

"This is a beautiful book that is very much needed."

— Rev. George T. Johnson, Ph.D., Former District Superintendent
United Methodist Church, New York City, NY

"...distills the wisdom of Dr. Mendes who has pioneered working with stress management. It is a practical, compassionate, nuts-and-bolts guide to understanding and reducing stress. The first of its kind, this easy-to-read manual will be treasured by all. "

— John E. Williams, Ph.D., Family Psychologist, Los Angeles, CA

iv

Acknowledgments

No one ever really writes a book all alone. There are always other people who help breathe life into any printed work. I have been blessed with many people who helped bring this book into existence.

I am grateful to Reverend Dr. Pelham Love, Senior Pastor of River Rouge Bible Assembly of Detroit, Michigan; the Reverend Doctor Arthur Davenport, my wonderful brother and Senior Pastor of First Church of God of Far Rockaway, New York and the late Reverend Doctor George Johnson, former Senior Pastor of Metropolitan United Methodist Church of New York City for their careful reading and critiquing of drafts of this manuscript. Each encouraged me and deepened my insight into *God's Stress Management Plan.* I owe a great deal to Dale Hill for her enthusiasm for this project and to my colleague and friend, Amelia Roberts, Ph.D., Associate Professor at the University of North Carolina at Chapel Hill for her spiritual and scholarly insights. My writing was greatly enhanced by the professional editing of Susan Titus Osborne and Jeri Love.

In many ways this book is a testimony of the ups and downs of my spiritual journey. I want to salute some of the people who have played major roles in my decades long effort to grow into the image of Christ. First among them was my deceased mother, Louise Davenport. Her profound love of God and the strength she drew from her relationship with Him, still inspires me. The Reverend William James was a towering spiritual giant in my youth. He ignited my thirst for knowledge of God and the principles of His kingdom. In my adult years my Sunday School teacher, Dr Tonya Lewis, showed me how practical the Christian faith is for overcoming life's challenges. I am truly privileged to be under the pastorate of Bishop Charles E. Blake of the West Angeles Church of God in Christ of Los Angeles, California. Bishop Blake is a gifted preacher who is called by God to motivate thousands of us to embrace the life-transforming Gospel of Jesus Christ.

Table of Contents

Foreword

I am highly honored and blessed to recommend *God's Stress Management Plan*, by Dr. Helen Mendes Love. As a pastor and a counselor, I am constantly confronted by people who are suffering with stress and its effects. Approximately eighty percent of our nation's population is afflicted with some kind of emotional or psychological malady or deficiency. The condition may be very mild, even unnoticeable, but the symptoms are there just the same.

Many people who seem to be "well off" externally are in internal agony and pain. All who are in that condition or wish to avoid it, would do well to read this book. *God's Stress Management Plan* teaches practical ways to obey the Great Commandments to love God with all of out hearts, souls minds and strength and to love other people, as we love ourselves. The book shows readers how by integrating these love commandments into their everyday lives, they will be equipped to avoid, reduce or better manage stress.

I have known Dr. Helen Mendes Love for many years. I have been blessed by her friendship and ministry. She is an able psychotherapist who is filled with the Spirit of God. God imparts His wisdom through her in this book and all who read it will be blessed.

Bishop Charles E. Blake
West Angeles Church of God in Christ

Prologue

"In the world you will have tribulations.
But be of good cheer, for
I have overcome the world."

John 16:33 (NKJV)

The needle stung as the nurse shoved it into my arm. *"Please Lord, help me,"* I prayed. I could hardly believe that this was happening to me. I came to the clinic for a quick fix of what I considered a minor discomfort.

"I feel pressure in my chest," I told the doctor.

As if translating my sentence from another language, the doctor told the nurse, "She has chest pains."

Turning to me, he said. "We are going to keep you in the hospital for a few days."

In my mind, I shouted, *"No! I don't have time for that."*

Aloud, I said. "Hospital? But I have a busy week ahead of me. Can I come back next week?"

Looking me steadily in the eye, the doctor said, "You may be having a heart attack."

My throat constricted, *"A heart attack?"* I felt the rush of blood to my head. The pressure in my chest grew worse.

"Maybe," he answered. "We're not sure. To be on the safe side, we want to hospitalize you and keep you under observation for two or three days."

Speechless, I slowly nodded my head. My mind flooded with memories of my parents, both of whom had heart attacks. My father had two attacks, each of which left him more disabled. Had my genetic legacy caught up with me?

"The Lord is near to all who call upon Him."
Psalm 145:18 (NIV)

My panic grew. I prayed more earnestly. Suddenly, I felt God's presence, and began to breathe slower. Silently I repeated the "Jesus Prayer."

**"Lord, Jesus Christ, Son of God,
Have mercy on me, my Savior."**

As I continued to repeat this prayer, my mind focused on God, not on the activities of the medical team as they prepared to hospitalize me. I grew calmer.

The nurse telephoned my husband, Gregory, who arrived before I was taken to the Cardiac Care Unit. He kissed me and held my hand.

Making a valiant attempt to keep the nervousness out of his voice, he asked, "What happened? How did you get here?"

"Thou wilt keep him in perfect peace whose mind is stayed on Thee."
Isaiah 26:3 (KJV)

I hesitated, trying to block out the urgent sounds of the emergency medical team rushing around, pushing carts, and pulling curtains around the beds of other patients. They spoke in reassuring tones to people who moaned in pain. I tried valiantly to ignore the return of my panic and the surge of shame I felt at being so vulnerable. I began to tell Gregory what happened. Halfway through, I burst into tears.

He tenderly stroked my hand. The comfort I drew from his love and his presence deepened when he said, "Let's pray." Gregory prayed aloud, interceding for me with God, the ultimate source of love, comfort, and healing.

"Again I say to you that if two of you agree on earth concerning anything that they ask, it will be done for them by My Father in heaven."
Matthew 18:19 (NKJV)

"Heavenly Father we come before You thanking and praising you for all that You are. We know that nothing is impossible for You. We ask that You touch Helen with Your peace and loving kindness.
We pray for the doctors. That You will guide them to find the proper diagnosis so that Helen's situation may be rectified. Heal her body. Give her Your comfort. Through Jesus Christ our Lord we pray. Amen."

"I, the Lord, thy God will hold thy right hand, saying unto thee fear not I will keep thee."
Isaiah 41:13 (KJV)

My fear diminished.

During the three days that I was hospitalized, my family, friends and prayer partners constantly prayed for me. In the quiet times, God spoke to my spirit and calmed my fears. I felt assured that no matter what my medical condition, He was with me. I, therefore, was at peace as doctors, nurses, and technicians poked, repeatedly drew blood samples and attached me to machines that told them things about me that I didn't know about myself.

Finally, after many tests, the doctors determined that I had not had a heart attack. However, they felt certain that the pressure in my chest was triggered by excessive stress, which sent my esophagus into spasms.

Inspite of my relief that I had not had a heart attack, I felt God urging me not to ignore the message which the spasms tried to commuicate to me. My body protested the great stresses with which I habitually lived as:

- ❖ A wife
- ❖ A mother of a son and daughter in the throes of adolescence.
- ❖ Chairperson of a major committee of my church, which was struggling to build a unified congregation of English, Spanish, Korean, and Tagalog speaking members.
- ❖ A full time, tenured professor at the University of Southern California, where I taught social work master degree and Ph.D. students how to help individuals, groups, and families with a range of psychological and social problems.
- ❖ Chairperson of several faculty committees.
- ❖ Psychotherapist, maintaining a thriving psycho-therapy practice where some of the clients I counseled had serious emotional problems.
- ❖ A public speaker, giving speeches and seminars to lay and professional audiences 35 - 40 times a year.

A month prior to my hospitalization, I resigned my tenured professor's position to work for myself full time.

In the whirl of all of these activities, I minimized the effects of my mounting stress, chronic fatigue and anxiety about the risks of giving up a secure job. Although I was earning more with my part time practice than my full time teaching position, I worried whether clients would continue to come. But the spasms shook me, literally and figuratively. I had to wake up and acknowledge the toll that stress was taking on my mind and body.

I alternated praying for God to help me and with scolding myself for eating too much, not exercising enough and resting too little. I wasn't afraid of dying. My worst fear was of becoming disabled. I thought of all the things I wanted to do, goals I wanted to achieve. I wanted to raise my children to be productive and responsible adults, to be a good wife, to be an excellent teacher, to truly help my clients, to make a lot of money, to be a good church leader. On and on went the list of goals and ambitions that motivated me. I thought that surely God wanted all of these things for me. That was the attitude with which I prayed. God should bless my worthy agenda!

In the middle of the night, I was suddenly awaken by memory of the Scripture, *"But seek first the Kingdom of God and His righteousness, and all these things shall be added to you."* **(Matthew 6:33)**.

Throughout the subsequent days, this Scripture reverberated through me. The more I meditated on it, the clearer it came to me that I was in this predicament *because my values and priorities were out of order!*

Later, during my quiet times with God, He showed me that although I used the gifts He gave me to help other people, my pride about this impaired my proper caring and loving of myself. As I took pleasure in my accomplishments and the admiration of others, my activities accelerated. As a result, my life became out of

> *"The eternal God is your refuge, and underneath are the everlasting arms."*
>
> **Deuteronomy 33:27 (NKJV)**

balance. God used my unexpected hospitalization to get my attention. I was so shaken that I felt forced to re-evaluate my relationship with Him, with others, and with myself. I felt certain that God wanted me to learn His way for His people to handle stress.

As a professor and therapist, I already had to keep abreast of the scientific literature on stress management. After my hospitalization, I began to diligently search the Bible to learn what God had to say about how we should manage stress. In *God's Stress Management Plan*, I focus on ten major principles undergirding God's plan for helping us avoid, reduce or better manage stress.

"God my Maker…gives songs in the night."

Job 35:10 (NKJV)

1
WHAT WE NEED TO KNOW ABOUT STRESS

*"...You formed my inward parts; ...I will praise
you for I am fearfully and wonderfully made."*
Psalm 139:13-14

Some people boast, "I'm too blessed to be stressed." They
seem to imply that living stress-free is always a good thing
and that one proof that we are blessed is that we won't ever be
stressed. The truth is that blessed or not, some degree of stress
is necessary for our growth, health and safety.

I define stress as mental and/or physical tension.
Frequently, the stress we experience is the prime motivation,
prompting us to give up bad habits, take better care of our
health, or to otherwise change and mature. For example,
when you were a toddler you, undoubtedly, experienced
some stress as you tried to comply with your parents'
demand that you give up the infantile pleasures of wetting
yourself anywhere and anytime you wanted. As an adult, the
concerns you feel about the potential threats to your life and
health motivates you to avoid driving your car at 110 miles an

hour, especially, along a darkened, unfamiliar road. As you can see, stress itself is not necessarily bad. In fact, it can be good for us.

It is when we experience too much of it for too long a time, that stress can harm us. God made us in such a way that when we regard something as a threat we feel what scientists call, a stress response. We mentally and physically experience tension when we perceive any threat to our safety, pride, prestige, control or anything that is important to us. In response to what we tell ourselves about any real and imagined threat, our bodies go through a series of biological changes to prepare us to fight or to escape.

The amount and intensity of our stress can be very important to our well being. If, for example, someone attempts to rob you at gunpoint, your mind will send an alarm signal to your body. Your sympathetic nervous system sends out a flood of hormonal messages, triggering dramatic increases in your heart rate and blood pressure. Your hearing becomes more acute. Your pupils' dilate to sharpen your vision. You may even start to perspire, even though your hands and feet become cold, as blood rushes from your extremities and from your digestive system. Your blood will speed on to your larger muscles needed to help you fight or run away. The amount and intensity of the stress you would feel in the above circumstances may be necessary to save your life.

However, the longer the time that level of stress lasts, the more potential harm it can do to you. Even if the attempted robbery (or any other trauma) lasts only a few minutes, you could go on thinking about it for months or even years. Each time you vividly remember and relive the trauma, you could trigger another mental and physical stress response.

Some of us have never been robbed, but our stress responses become triggered when we perceive that someone or something hurts our feelings, challenges our self-esteem, our desire to be in control and the like. We can trigger our mind-body alarm system whenever we obsess about the bad things that can happen to us or our love ones. If our stress responses are frequently triggered or go on for long periods of time, we can become ill. Stress that goes on for a long time is called Chronic Stress.

Chronic Stress

Researchers have found that people who live with Chronic Stress are more likely to develop:

Hypertension	**Asthma**
Colitis	**Bronchitis**
Chronic diarrhea	**Diabetes**
Peptic ulcers	**Osteoporosis**
Infertility	**Headaches**
Sexual frigidity	**Muscle tensions**

In short, Chronic Stress can make us very sick.

Anger is another common form of Chronic Stress. If you have been angry and resentful with someone for a long time, or if you tend to harbor resentments, your body will adapt to a higher level of arousal. Your blood

"Let all bitterness, wrath, anger, clamor and evil speaking, be put away from you with all malice...."
Ephesians 4:31 (NKJV)

3

pressure goes up and will not easily come down. Your blood vessels cannot tolerate elevated blood pressure for long periods of time without seriously damaging your health.

> *"Do not let the sun go down on your wrath."*
> **Ephesians 4:26 (NKJV)**

Traumatic Stress

Unlike Chronic Stress, Traumatic Stress can happen suddenly. We could experience Traumatic Stress when for example:

- ❖ Someone we love is murdered or otherwise suddenly dies.
- ❖ We, or people we care about, become seriously injured in an accident.
- ❖ Terrorists attack our country.
- ❖ Earthquakes, fires, floods or other disasters destroy our homes.
- ❖ We are assaulted, robbed or raped.

When the stresses traumatize us, it will take longer than normal for us to regain our composure and to turn off our stress alarm system.

If we can't turn off our alarm responses after approximately six months, it is likely that we are experiencing a Post-traumatic Stress Disorder (PTSD).

Post-traumatic Stress Disorder

People who have PTSD tend to continually re-experience the traumatic event long after it occurred. They frequently have flashbacks and/or nightmares about the event. For example:

Mary was alone when she was suddenly awakened by three robbers, who broke into her home. They plundered her

4

house. All three of the men raped her. For almost a year after this event, Mary had difficulty falling and staying asleep. She had nightmares. She insisted that her husband or someone else always be at home with her, and she became extremely anxious whenever she was at home alone for even ten minutes. After the trauma, she was often irritable and had uncharacteristic outbursts of anger.

Not everyone has an immediate and on-going response to trauma as did Mary. As we have seen with war veterans, some people don't experience the symptoms of Post-traumatic Stress Disorder until six months or more after the trauma. PTSD can be all the more distressing because it often seems to "come out of nowhere."

Eustress

Not all stress comes from "bad" experiences. Stress responses can also be triggered by "good" things. This is called *Eustress.* Anyone who has planned a wedding, had a baby she wanted, received a promotion, bought a new house, or unexpectedly inherited a lot of money knows that these "good" experiences can also trigger fears about one's adequacy, worthiness, or ability to cope with these "blessings." Inherent in all of these good stressors is the need for change. If you don't like changes, you will probably experience various degrees of stress as you make the adjustments required to accommodate your blessings.

Some of us thrive on Eustress. Perhaps, like me, you feel exhilarated when you are challenged to reach new goals or overcome obstacles to your achievements. As every athlete knows, a certain level of stress enhances strength, concentration, and productivity. A surge of adrenaline can make the difference in whether or not he or she wins the race.

"Do you not know that those who run in a race all run, but one receives the prize? Run in such a way that you may obtain it."

1 Corinthians 9:24 (NKJV)

But eustress is only good, if it is short-lived. Some of us become addicted to our adrenaline and the high it produces. We love living highly competitive and fast-paced lives. As my hospitalization taught me years ago, if we stay hyped for too long, eustress can harm us.

REMEMBER

1. We can live with stress for so long that it feels natural. Prolonged stress can be harmful.

2. If you experienced a significant trauma, you may be at risk of experiencing traumatic stress or Post-Traumatic Stress Disorder.

3. Even good experiences can cause stress, especially when they require significant changes in your life.

4. Be aware of the presence and quantity of stress in your life.

2
ASSESS YOUR STRESS

"Therefore take heed to your spirit"
Malachi 2:16 (NKVJ)

Sources of stress are not always obvious. Many times a number of seemly "little things" can, when added together, deliver a major jolt to our nervous systems. Things that stress us today may reactivate feelings we had about painful events in our past. At such times, it may seem that we are over-reacting. In reality, we are responding simultaneously to the present and to the past. For example, your current conflicts with your boss may reactivate painful feelings about fights you had with your brother, years ago.

Mental health professionals find that by assessing experiences you have had during the past twenty- four months, you can often gain more insights than if you only considered what is currently going on in your life.

Prayerfully, examine whether any of the following sources of stress have occurred in your life, during the past twenty-four months. (Some of you may want to reflect on longer time periods, especially if you have chronic stress.)

POSSIBLE SOURCES OF STRESS

I. Physical Health Problems

Your body is involved in all of your life experiences. Therefore, its health is a major factor influencing the quality of your life.

Within the past 24 months, have you experienced stress from any of the following:

- ❖ Chronic health problems?
- ❖ New symptoms? If yes, do you or your doctor know what caused them?
- ❖ Newly diagnosed health problems?
- ❖ Deteriorating health conditions?
- ❖ Being hospitalized?
- ❖ Having to take medications for your health problems?

2. Mental or Emotional Problems

Your mental and emotional health plays important roles in determining the quality of your overall health and well being.

Have you experienced stress from any of the following:

- ❖ Chronic mental and/or emotional problems?
- ❖ New symptoms? If so, do you know what causes them?
- ❖ Newly diagnosed emotional or mental conditions?
- ❖ Deteriorating conditions?
- ❖ Being hospitalized for observation or treatment?
- ❖ Being seen for outpatient therapy?

❖ Taking medication for your mental and/or emotional problem?

3. Relationship Problems

Problems in relationships are usually obvious sources of stress. However, we may underestimate their impacts, especially if they have gone on for a long time or we have several conflicted relationships.

During the past two years, have you experienced stress from any of the following:

A. Conflicts with your:
❖ current or former spouse or lover?
❖ children?
❖ stepchildren?
❖ parents?
❖ in-laws?
❖ siblings?
❖ spouse's former mate or lover?

B. Changes in your family life such as:
❖ you, your spouse or lover became pregnant?
❖ the birth of your child?
❖ your spouse began working outside the home?
❖ your spouse or lover became unemployed?
❖ a member of your family became ill or his/her condition deteriorated?
❖ a family member abuses drugs and/or alcohol?

9

❖ you take care of an aged relative, including in-laws?

C. Losses such as:

❖ infidelity? (Yours or your spouse's or lover's.)

❖ separation(s)?

❖ reconciliation(s) (i.e., trying again.)?

❖ you fell out of love with your spouse or lover?

❖ divorce or otherwise ending an important relationship?

❖ your child leaves home?

❖ Death of your:

> spouse or lover?

> parent, including in-law?

> child?

❖ You or your spouse had a miscarriage?

> an abortion?

4. Eustress

Even events that we normally regard as good can be sources of stress. The occurrences of these good things may require us to change in order to accommodate them into our lives. Change can be stressful.

Examining the past two years, have you:

❖ fallen in love?

❖ begun a romantic relationship?

❖ successfully lost a lot of weight?

❖ adopted a child?

❖ had a child to get married?

❖ become a grandparent?

5. Problems at Work

Those of us who have jobs spend most of our waking hours at work. Consequently, work-related experiences have enormous effects on our levels of stress. Looking back at the past two years, have any of the following been sources of stress for you?

❖ You dislike or have been bored with your job?

❖ You lost your job?

❖ You've had difficulty finding work?

❖ You've started a new job?

❖ Your employer's policies and procedures are unfair or confusing?

❖ Your salary is inadequate?

❖ You have a high-risk job?

❖ There have been changes in your work schedule or working conditions?

❖ You have a difficult boss?

❖ There are conflicts between your work and family responsibilities?

❖ A co-worker you like leaves the job?

❖ You have conflicts with a co-worker?

❖ You retired or will retire within the coming months?

6. Financial Problems

It is not unusual for people to feel stressed about money. Most often they are stressed because they believe that they lack the money they want or need. It is also possible for people to feel stressed by a sudden increase in their income.

Have you experienced any of the following within the past two years?

❖ A significant increase in income?

❖ A significant decrease in income?

❖ A significant decrease in savings/assets?

❖ A significant increase in debts?

❖ Letters and phone calls from creditors?

❖ Bankruptcy?

❖ Tax problems?

❖ Eviction?

❖ Lawsuit?

7. Problems in Your Physical Environment

Many times we underestimate the degree to which our physical environment can be sources of stress.

Do you regard the environment in which you live as:

❖ dangerous?

❖ crowded?

❖ noisy?

❖ dirty, ugly or disorderly?

8. Problems with your Spiritual Environment

Sometimes the spiritual organizations in which you participate can add to rather than relieve your stress.

Have you had any of the following experiences within the past twenty-four months?

❖ You have been attending a spiritually dead church?

❖ The pastor/leader has had personal problems that has been impairing his/her leadership?

❖ There has been a turn over in the leadership?

❖ There have been serious conflicts among church members?

Count the total numbers of sources of stress that you have experienced. If you have had five or more in the recent past, you are in danger of having excessive stress. Which areas of your life are most stressful? How do you feel about them? Write your thoughts and feelings in a journal. Pray about them.

When I did this assessment fifteen years ago, I identified nine things that were sources of stress for me. They were:

1. Chronic physical health problem—I had high blood pressure.

2. New physical symptoms—My doctor told me that I was "sugar sensitive" an early sign that I was developing Adult Onset Type II Diabetes.

3. New mental/emotional health problems—I had increased anxiety because I had given my resignation from a tenured professorship, in order to work for myself.

4. Family conflicts—Parenting my teenage son was very difficult for me.

5. Work Life—A colleague was murdered by his wife, whom I liked very much.

6. Work Life —I was going to change employment in a few months.

7. Finances—I had a significant increase in income from my psychotherapy and consulting practice. Coming from a lower socio-economic background

did not give me adequate tools for managing this eustress.

8. Spiritual—I attended, what for me, was a spiritually dead church. This was excruciating.

9. Spiritual—There were significant conflicts among church members.

Clearly, my nine sources of stress contributed to the excessive stress that landed me in the hospital!

Now that you have counted the number and sources of your stress, consider how you function with your stress. Each of us needs to learn what are our individual symptoms of excessive stress.

ASSESS YOUR SYMPTOMS OF EXCESSIVE STRESS

I. Mental and Emotional Symptoms

Do you or other people notice that you are prone to be:

❖ Irritable?

❖ Depressed?

❖ Anxious?

❖ Worried about a lot of things?

❖ Easily angered?

❖ Jealous?

❖ Forgetful?

❖ Overly suspicious or paranoid?

❖ Indecisive?

❖ Tearful?

❖ A perfectionist?

❖ A procrastinator?

❖ Delusional (i.e., you distort what you see or hear)?

❖ Desperate?

❖ Hopeless?

❖ Suicidal?

❖ Accident prone?

❖ Homicidal?

❖ Other symptoms? (specify)

2. Physical Symptoms

How often do you experience:

❖ Headaches?

❖ Rapid heart palpitations?

❖ Tension (i.e., tense muscles, grinding teeth, etc)?

❖ Sweaty palms?

❖ Shallow breathing?

❖ Fatigue?

❖ Difficulty falling or staying asleep?

❖ Loss of appetite?

❖ Chronic pain?

❖ High blood pressure?

❖ Stomach upset or other gastrointestinal problems?

❖ Dizzy spells?

❖ Sexual impotence or frigidity?

❖ Hives or other skin eruptions?

❖ Cold or other respiratory conditions?

❖ Substance abuse (alcohol, prescribed or illegal drugs)?

❖ Other (specify)?

3. Social Relationships Symptoms

Do any of the following describe you?

❖ Avoid people?

❖ Have difficulty getting along with two or more people?

❖ Keep your problems to yourself and try to work them out on your own?

❖ Almost never ask others for help?

4. Work-related Symptoms

You spend the majority of your waking hours working. Do you often:

❖ Feel bored or hate your job?

❖ Make too many mistakes?

❖ Feel that you are not doing the work God intends for you to do?

5. Financial Symptoms

How you handle money can cause or reveal your level of stress. Do you often:

❖ Lack money to pay your bills?

❖ Spend money to feel better?

❖ Gamble?

❖ Worry about money?

6. Spiritual Symptoms

Your spiritual life affects the overall quality of your life. Do you find that you often:

❖ Can't pray?

❖ Rarely pray?

❖ Don't trust God?

❖ Feel angry with God?

❖ Feel alienated from God?

❖ Feel that God is punishing or persecuting you?

❖ Feel persecuted by Satan and/or demons?

❖ Worry about your salvation?

❖ Feel unloved by God?

❖ Hate God?

❖ Sin?

❖ Feel guilty about your sins?

❖ Hold grudges against other people?

❖ Other (specify)?

How many symptoms of stress have your identified as spoiling your experience of an abundant life? Write what you think and feel about them in your journal. Pray about them. Ask The Lord to help you to learn and follow His plan so that you can have a more stress-resistant life.

REMEMBER

1. Too much stress makes life a mess.

2. Pay regular attention to the specific things that stress you.

3. Be aware of the physical, mental, emotional, social and spiritual symptoms that indicate that you have too much stress in your life.

4. Integrate into your life-style God's plan for helping you avoid, reduce or better manage stress.

God's Stress Management Plan

3

GOD'S STRESS MANAGEMENT PLAN

"For I know the plans I have for you,"
declared the Lord, "Plans to prosper
you and not to harm you, plans to
give you hope and a future."
Jeremiah 29:11 (NIV)

God has plans for us. The core of His plan is love. Love has the power to banish the fears that cause most of our stresses (1 John 4:18). To tap into this awesome power, we need to receive God's unconditional love, love Him passionately in return, and sincerely love other people and ourselves. (Matthew 22:37 - 40)

Through our love connections with God, we have access to His infinite resources to help us manage our lives. When we ask for His help, God replaces our fears, not only with love, but with power and with sound minds. (2 Timothy 1:7)

"But those who wait upon the Lord shall renew their strength; They shall mount up with wings like eagles. They shall run and not be weary, They shall walk and not faint."
Isaiah 40:31 (NKJV)

Empowered by our love venture with God, we become better able to have healthy love relationships with other people. Research shows that people who have good relationships with others, handle stress and recover from its damage better than people who do not. Healthy love connections with others allow us to receive and to give affection, comfort, and practical help to deal with a variety of stressful experiences.

"Love never fails."
Cor. 13:8 (NKJV)

Our fervent love relationships with God, enables us to develop godly self-love. God loves you, and He also wants you to love yourself (Matthew 22:39). In fact, healthy self-love is crucial to obeying Christ, who taught us to love other people **as** we love ourselves (Matthew 22:39). In other words, the love that you and I have for other people should be equivalent to the quantity, quality, and extent of our self-love.

The high standard for this proper love of ourselves and others is described in 1 Corinthians 13:4-8. Only in partnership with God can you and I ever hope to love ourselves and others like that. When we love ourselves as God wants us to, we can then draw upon the strength that comes from self-respect and healthy self-esteem.

Since my hospitalization in 1985, I have been learning to integrate into my life God's principles for equipping me to better deal with stress. I have enthusiastically taught hundreds of clients, seminar participants, and friends how to apply these powerful principles to their own stress-filled lives.

"[God] comforts us in all our tribulation, that we may be able to comfort those who are in any trouble."
2 Corinthians 1:4 (NKJV)

20

People who integrated these love principles into their lives tell me that they have achieved levels of peace and well being that they never knew

"Fear not, for I am with you;..."

Isaiah 41:10 (NKJV)

before. Many of their stories, in addition to my own, are included in this book. I have changed their names and any other data that might reveal their identities. Their stories help to illustrate, in very practical ways, why and how we should implement God's stress management plan.

This book differs from other books written about stress in that it focuses on the power of love in the effective management of stress. The chapters that follow are guides for how to integrate God's love plan into your life and thereby become better equipped to:

1. **Avoid** the stresses that result from sinning. Not only does our sinful behaviors take us outside of God's will for our lives, but sooner or later they bring hosts of problems that grieve us, our families, and friends. The Bible teaches us God's principles for

   "I delight to do Your will, O my God."

   Psalm 40:8 (NKJV)

   how to avoid the pitfalls that ensnare and distress those who disobey Him. When we love God, we eagerly obey His principles and avoid the troubles that disobedience brings.

2. **Reduce** the negative impacts of the stresses that we inevitable experience in the wear and tear of everyday life. The impact that stress has on us is greatly influenced by our attitudes, and our self-talk, and the decisions we make as a result. The impact is also influenced by the spiritual, social, personal, and tangible resources we draw upon to deal with the stress. The stronger our love

relationships with God, other people, and ourselves, the more potent are the resources we can bring to bear on the stresses we encounter.

3. **Manage** the stresses induced by catastrophic events. The stresses of rape, the death of loved ones, accidents that cause permanent damage to the body, chronic illnesses, financial ruin, and the like can so easily overwhelm us. But God has promised to be with us even in the midst of such tragedies. As we accept and return His love and become channels of His love to others, God gives us His peace, which surpasses our ability to understand. (Philippians 4:6-7) His unique peace can preserve our sanity and empower us to manage what might otherwise be unmanageable.

It is my prayer that this book will help you master Ten Principles of *God's Stress Management Plan*, so that you will prosper and not be harmed. And that you will face whatever the circumstances of your life, with hope, that is grounded in Him.

"Fear not, for I am with you; ...Be not dismayed, for I am your God. I will strengthen you, Yes, I will help you. I will uphold you with My righteous right hand."

Isaiah 41:10 (NKJV)

TEN BIBLICAL PRINCIPLES FOR AVOIDING, REDUCING OR BETTER MANAGING STRESS

Principle 1

FIRST, SEEK THE KINGDOM

"You shall have no other gods before me."

Exodus 20:3 (NKJV)

I learned that I had invited stress into my life when my priorities were out of order. I was diligently pursuing what appeared to be worthy but worldly goals. I loved God but He needed me to see that He was not at the center of my life. For example:

I often rushed around in pursuit of success and money. In the process, I pushed God to the periphery of my life. Perhaps like I did, you also tend to think about God when you are at church, while you say grace or when you are in trouble. Just as human relationships deteriorate when there is little or no meaningful interactions or communications, so, too, they damage our relationships with God.

False Gods and Stress

The Bible taught me that God, the Maker and Sustainer of all life, wants us to take Him very seriously. He promises to bless those who give Him His rightful place and punish those who do not. (Exodus 20:5-6) Therefore, the fundamental principle for managing stress is to **LOVE GOD FIRST**. He is to have first place in our lives. *"You shall have no other gods before* me...For I, the Lord your God am a jealous God...." **(Exodus 20:3,5) (NKJV)**

"Thou shalt worship the Lord thy God and Him only shalt thou serve."

Matthew 4:10 (KJV)

When this first commandment was given to the Israelites, they lived among people who worshiped many different gods. Today's Christians also live among people who worship different gods. We contemporary Christians might be inclined to be smug, thinking that we are in no danger of worshipping false gods. But that is not true.

I know people who accepted Christ as their Savior and Lord and regard themselves as Christians. Yet they cling to beliefs in the powers of the Hindu, Santeria, animistic or voodoo gods they worshipped prior to accepting Christ. For example:

Olatungi, a Nigerian, who lived and studied in the United States, believed that he was a very devout Christian. However, when he had a financial crisis he became acutely anxious. He poured libations and prayed to a deity he learned to worship in his childhood. His money problems worsened. So did his upset stomach, shallow breathing and insomnia.

A number of other Christians attempt to integrate various non-biblical theologies into Christianity. Whether it is "New Age" theology, metaphysics, astrology or ancient mysticism, what often happens is that the attempted integration, actually adulterates the person's Christian beliefs and practices. For example:

Moriah regularly worships at a church where the minister teaches about an all-accepting god who loves uncon-

26

ditionally and never punishes anyone. As a result of this feel-good theology, Moriah's attitudes and behaviors often violate biblical teachings. She frequently complains about emotional and bodily tensions, loneliness, and depression.

Children sometimes have school-mates who are Satan worshippers. In their curiosity and desire to fit in with their peers, some of these youths experiment with satanic rituals and worship. The conflicts, which many of these

"Train up a child in the way he should go, And when he is old he will not depart from it."

Proverbs 22:6 (NKJV)

young people have with their parents and other authorities, exacerbate the stress of their adolescence. Christian parents become distressed and confused by their children's new allegiances and activities. These disintegrating families try valiantly to manage their anxieties by clinging to the hope that their children will outgrow this phase of their development.

Most of us would not be inclined to worship the gods of other religions. But we, nevertheless, can make "gods" of our work, spouse, children, social status,

"Set your affection on things above, not on things on the earth."

Colossians 3:2 (KJV)

money, material possessions, and the like. Anything that we greatly esteem and give power over our lives can take God's rightful place. For instance:

Camille came to see me because of her immobilizing depression. Between her sobs, she told me how desperate she felt. "I think that Ralph doesn't love me anymore. In the first years of our marriage, he loved me so much. We were so happy. It was heaven. Now I panic each time he becomes silent. When he doesn't talk to me I get so scared that he's mad at me and has stopped loving me. "And if he has," she

*gasped, barely containing her hysteria, "then I don't want
to go on living." Recently, the number of her "accidental"
falls has increased. So has her drinking.*

Camille has given her husband God's place in her life.
She is so dependent upon Ralph that without his love and
approval she feels that she has no
reason to live.

Some popular love songs
encourage us to make gods of the
people we love. If you make a god of
someone you will find that your sense
of security is easily shaken by any
threat to your relationship with this
other imperfect human being.

Songs, such as "I Did It My Way,"
encourage us to obey our own wills
rather than God's. When you become
your own god, you become vulnerable
to any perceived threats to your sense
of control, pride, or status. A vaunted
self-image inevitably damages your
relationships with others who are
offended by your arrogance. They
eventually grow to dislike you.

*"As for man, his days
are like grass; As a
flower of the field so
he flourishes. For the
wind passes over it
and it is gone, And its
place remembers it no
more. But the mercy
of the Lord is from
everlasting to
everlasting on those
who fear Him. And
His righteousness to
children's children; To
such as keep His
covenant, and to those
who remember His
commandments to do
them."*

Psalm 103:15-18 (NKJV)

Stress and Hating God

Some people's stress results from disliking or even hating
God. I have found that people who hate the Lord God fall into
three categories. There are those who:

28

1. **Disapprove of God.** These people are especially angry that God has definite standards of right and wrong, by which He judges us and sometimes punishes us. Some of them may also disapprove of God's plan for salvation, thinking that it is not inclusive and is unfair. (John 3:16) *"I don't want to worship such a God,"* they say. These people are deeply offended that God does not conform to their ideas of what He should be like. Consequently, they do not want to have anything to do with Him.

   "For my thoughts are not your thoughts, nor are your ways My ways, says the Lord"

   Isaiah 55:8 (NKJV)

2. **Are Disappointed with God.** People in this category may have had a more positive relationship with God in the past, but now hold grudges against Him.

   "I prayed and begged God to let my child live, but He took her anyway," said Ted. With great bitterness toward God, he declared, "I'll never pray to Him again!"

   Like Ted, some people are so angry and unforgiving of God that they even curse Him. They have closed their hearts to Him and have no use for Him.

3. **Displace Their Hatred of Others Onto God.** Some people have had painfully disappointing experiences with parents or others who professed to be Christians. One man told about his friend who is now in prison for armed robbery. The prisoner remembers his father's rages during which he "quoted the Bible with whiskey breath." One night, the son took a knife to his father's neck to

protect a younger brother from being beaten to death. Like this son, some people hate their "religious" parents and abhor anything or anyone that is associated with God. In a sense, we can say that God gets a "bum rap." Nevertheless, the person hates God.

If you hate God, you are not only forfeiting His blessings, but are inviting His punishments. Although it is unpopular among some Christians to acknowledge and reflect upon God's anger and jealousy, the Bible clearly states that He is not only loving but He is also a jealous God who can become angry (Exodus 20:5; Jeremiah 13:15-17; Romans 1:18).

Nothing seems to make Him angrier than His people failing to love Him and give Him first place in their lives. As a jealous God, He bestows or allows the perversity, evil, mischief or fault of those who hate Him (i.e., are His enemies) to fall upon their children, grandchildren, great grand-children, and even the great great grandchildren (Exodus 20:5). All of us have heard about or perhaps are even members of families that have been "dysfunctional" for generations. There are families, for instance, where incest, alcoholism and family violence can be traced back to the great great grandparents. Undoubtedly, some of these stresses are the intergenerational punishments of forebearers who hated God.

Thus we can only conclude that God is very serious about us loving Him and putting Him first in our lives.

Fortunately by making God our first love, and accepting His Son, Jesus Christ, we help reverse the intergenerational curse.

HOW TO MAKE GOD
YOUR FIRST PRIORITY

God asks, "May I reign over you? May I be the top priority in your life?" If our answer is "no," "maybe," or "sure, but only every once in a while," then nothing else in our lives will line up as they should. Our emotions, health, and relationships will be off center. And stress becomes our constant companion.

To give God His proper place in our lives we need to:

1.   Begin each day with thoughts of Him. I greet the Lord each morning with a prayer. In later chapters we will discuss the importance of prayer more fully. At this point, I want to emphasize the importance of beginning your day with thoughts about God. You could, for example, simply pray, *"Good morning, Lord. Thank you for allowing me to wake up this morning. Help me to remember that You will be with me throughout this coming day. Help me to live this day so that others may see Your presence in my life. Amen."*

> *"As for me, I will call upon God, And the Lord shall save me. Evening and morning and at noon I will pray, and He shall hear my voice."*
> **Psalm 55:16-17 (NKJV)**

2.   Study, at least, one verse of Scripture every day. Read the inspirational stories of King David, Job, Queen Esther, Daniel, the Apostle Paul, and others for whom God was first priority. Learn who God is and how a strong love relationship with Him is your best insurance against chronic stress.

> *"Seek and you shall find."*
> **Matthew 7:7 (NKJV)**

Each morning as I eat breakfast I digest the word of God contained in *Our Daily Bread*, a booklet of scriptures and meditations. (See Appendix A for

31

how to obtain free copies of this insightful aid to your spiritual growth .)

3. As you make decisions, seek God's will. Pray for guidance. Analyze the values underlying your decisions, actions, ambitions, and what you communicate. See to it that your values are aligned with God's. Evangelist Tim Storey advises that when making decisions, we should seek the "God idea" not merely the "good idea."

4. Memorize Exodus 20:3-5. Let it be a guide for you.

    You shall have no other gods before me....you shall not serve them. For I, the Lord your God, am a jealous God, visiting the iniquity of the fathers upon the children to the third and fourth generations of those who hate Me.

REMEMBER

To locate God's place in your life ask yourself:

1. Where is God on the list of my priorities?

2. What would a review of how I use my time, talents and money reveal about how important God is to me?

3. Are there people in my life who I try to please more than I try to please God? Who are they?

4. Do I try to integrate non-biblical theologies into my Christian beliefs and practices? Which ones?

5. Could any of the stress I experience be caused by my putting other things, people, or activities before loving and obeying God?

6. What specific steps will I take to insure that God has first place in my life?

After answering these questions, spend some time reflecting on the place God occupies in your life. In a journal write what you believe that God is saying to you about your love for Him and the place that you have allotted Him in your life.

We've looked at how failing to love God and failing to put Him first can make us more vulnerable to stress. Now let us look at how welcoming His love helps us to avoid, reduce and better manage stress.

Principle 2
ACCEPT GOD'S LOVE

"God is Love"
1 John 4:8 (NKJV)

God loves you and has a wonderful plan for your life. (Jeremiah 29:11-12) He wants only the highest good for you and me. His plans are full of gifts for us.

God's Gift of the Natural World

His gifts offer us innumerable ways to better manage our stress. God has placed a generous supply of stress-relieving resources in our natural environment.

For example, any of us can better handle stress, if we take time to:

❖ Spend a few moments really looking at trees, or plants in bloom.

❖ Enjoy the caress of a gentle breeze.

❖ Smell the scent of the ocean, mountain air, or the aroma of a favorite fruit.

❖ Listen to water lapping against the shore, a breeze rustling through the leaves of trees, the conversations of crickets, or the laughter of children.

"Bless the Lord, O my soul; ...who satisfies your mouth with good things, so that your youth is renewed like the eagles."

Psalm 103:1,5 (NKJV)

❖ Slowly taste a delicious fruit. Savor nuts, grains, and raw vegetables. Really enjoy the pleasure of their tastes and textures.

❖ Leisurely soak away muscle tensions in a tub of warm water.

❖ Let the steam in a shower, or a Jacuzzi, or an outdoor hot springs melt away bodily strains.

❖ Surround ourselves with green and blue colors. They help us to feel calmer and more relaxed. You could, for example, decorate your home or office with green plants. Or you could spend time outdoors, lying in the grass or resting beneath a leafy tree.

❖ Cultivate a garden or grow house plants. Working with soil can be immensely satisfying and relaxing.

❖ Soothe away stress by taking a warm mud bath.

❖ Watch a sunset and let its ever-shifting red, orange, and gold colors distract us from stressful thoughts.

❖ Observe a sunrise. Let the dawn remind us that "God's mercy is new every morning."

❖ Sit in a garden and delight our senses with mingled fragrances of different flowers and their profusion of colors.

❖ Slowly sip hot stress reducing Chamomile tea.

❖ Get a pet. Our relationships with pets can be tremendous stress relievers.

God did not have to make the natural world so beautiful and restorative. But He did. Enjoy this blessing and let it help reduce your stress.

His Supreme Gift of Love

It is astonishing that God loves us in spite of our imperfections. He, however, does not love our sinful behaviors, thoughts, and attitudes. In fact, because He is Holy, He hates sin. Although every human can enjoy the natural world that He has created (Romans 1:19-20; Psalm 19:1), we cannot on our own have an intimate eternal relationship with Him. Our addiction to sin spiritually separates us from God. Sin creates a barrier which we are ill-equipped to dismantle. But God wants to have a passionate love relationship with you and me. So He established a wonderful way to have that happen.

He sent His Son, Jesus Christ, to dismantle that barrier by taking upon Himself the penalties that we deserve for our sins (1 John 4:9-12).

> *"...God demonstrated His own love toward us, in that while we were yet sinners, Christ died for us..."*
>
> **Romans 5:8 (NKJV)**

But we have a part in whether we will personally benefit from His sacrifice. We become eligible for God's special benefits program when we individually make the decision to believe in Christ's divinity, teachings, and in the redemptive power of his death and resurrection. This means that we each choose, as an act of our will, to accept Christ as our Savior and Lord. When we choose to relate to God through Jesus Christ we become adopted into God's family as sons and daughters (Ephesians 1:5; John 1:12). Then we know and experience God's love on a personal level.

If you have not already done so, choose to receive Christ now. Talk to God, i.e., pray, and tell Him that you accept the supreme manifestation of His love for you —Jesus Christ and the work of Christ's redeeming death and resurrection. Don't worry about how to pray. God knows your heart. He is less concerned with your words than He is with the attitude of your heart. The following is a suggested prayer.

"If thou shalt confess with thy mouth the Lord Jesus and shalt believe in thine heart that God hath raised Him from the dead, thou shalt be saved."

Romans 10:9 (KJV)

"Holy Father, thank you for loving me, in spite of my sins. I accept Your Supreme Gift of Love, Your Son, Jesus Christ.

Lord Jesus, thank You for dying on the cross that my sins may be forgiven and that I might have eternal life. I open my heart to You and accept You as my Savior and Lord. I surrender control of the throne of my life to You.

Holy Spirit help me to be transformed into the person God wants me to be. Amen."

How Accepting Jesus Helps With Stress

One of the two immediate benefits of our new relationship with God is that all of our sins are forgiven (John 3:16).

Almost all of us, at some point in our lives, have felt the distress of a guilty conscience, and know that it sometimes can be extremely stressful. People use a variety of methods to relieve the torments of guilt. These methods can include apologizing or attempting to make up for our wrongs through some act of atonement.

"I, even I, Am He who blots out your transgressions for My own sake; and I will not remember your sins."

Isaiah 43:25 (NKJV)

Others attempt to mollify their troublesome consciences by rationalizing their wrong doings or blaming others. For example:

Sixty-three years old Ed finds life empty and lonely. Periodically he telephones his adult daughters in search of family warmth. One of his three daughters occasionally invites him for a family dinner. At these gatherings, his two other daughters barely speak to him, and exclude him from the love and affection they show to other family members.

"As far as the east is from the west, so far hath He removed our transgressions from us."

Psalm 103:12 (NKJV)

Years ago, before his wife died, she told him that his daughters said that when they were children, he repeatedly abused them sexually. He became enraged at this accusation and vehemently denied them to his wife. Now when he is alone in his apartment, he occasionally has flash backs of his late night prowls into the bedrooms of his daughters. These guilt-stained memories are shoved out of consciousness as Ed tells himself how his wife's frigidity drove him to seek the bodies of his children. "None of this would have happened," he tells himself, "if she would have been more loving to me."

Unlike Ed, other people may accept responsibilities for their wrong doings but don't know how to make amends. They may try to blot out their guilt by compulsively doing "good" deeds in an unconscious effort to atone. Some use work in an attempt to distract themselves from the incessant demands of their guilt and shame. There are women and men who try to flee their emotional and mental torments through self-destructive behaviors, such as sexual promiscuity, drug and alcohol abuse, homicide, or even suicide. Needless to say these behaviors greatly multiple the stresses in their lives and in the lives of their families and friends.

God has arranged it so that we can live our lives with the special peace that comes from knowing that the things we did wrong before accepting Jesus Christ have been forever pardoned. (Colosians 2:13-14) I know that I am personally very grateful for that forgiveness. Knowing that God has released me from the punishment my sin deserves enables me to forgive and accept myself; thus increasing my self-esteem and self-love. My gratitude to God makes me eager to forgive others who offend me.

Whenever we sin after accepting Christ, we need only to sincerely repent. We no longer need to be burdened with guilt or shame, because He faithfully forgives us (1 John 1:9).

The second immediate benefit of accepting Jesus Christ and thereby establishing a new relationship with God is that you will have eternal life (John 3:16-18). In this life and beyond, you will have an intensely loving relationship with God. This covenant addresses one of life's major stressors — death.

"Thanks be unto God for His unspeakable gift"
2 Corinthians 9:15 (KJV)

This promise greatly helped me many years ago. I was in church and crying profusely. Every now and then, I paused and stared with disbelief at the casket in which my sister lay. I kept remembering how startled I was a week earlier when my telephone rang at 4:23 a.m.

Barely awake I said, "Hello?"

"Aunt Helen?" my niece Irene asked, trying to steady her voice.

39

I grew apprehensive. "Yes?" I said.

"Mother is dead." Irene sobbed.

Fully awake and not wanting to believe what I heard, I asked, "What did you say?"

"Mother is dead." Between her sobs, Irene told me about the car accident, which took the life of her mother, my beloved sister.

At her funeral, I again felt the sharp pain of losing her. I fought accepting that we would never ever laugh together again. I resisted the idea that I would never again listen with rapt attention to the stories she was so gifted in telling. So I cried out loud. Looking in my direction, the minister said, "If you're crying, you're crying for yourself."

His admonishment had little effect on me. I went on crying. I felt that it was okay for me to feel sorry for myself. After all, I had lost the sister who was like a junior mother to me.

"If you're crying, you're crying for yourself," he repeated. "Ruth has gone to be with the Lord," he said. "She's in Heaven with God." Now he had my attention! I stopped crying so that I could hear him better.

> "Having now been justified by His blood, we shall be saved from wrath through Him."
> Romans 5:9 (NKJV)

"Ruth is happy now. Her life here on earth was hard. Now she is full of joy, because she is with her heavenly Father," the minister said.

As I listened, I thought about how heart broken she'd been about her unhappy marriage during the last two years of her life. The minister reminded me that because Ruth had accepted Jesus Christ, God's supreme gift of love, she would spend eternity in God's holy and loving presence. That thought brought me immense comfort. My grief was outweighed by my happiness that she is with God. Through the years, that belief has played an enormous role in helping me to heal from this major loss.

> *"Neither death, nor life...nor height, nor depth, nor any other creature shall be able to separate us from the love of God."*
> **Romans 8:38, 39 (KJV)**

Over the years I have met many Christians who faced their own or a loved one's death with calmness because they anticipated that they or their loved one would spend eternity with God.

God is the quintessential Good Father (Matthew 7:11b; Psalm 103:13). As the Father, He blesses and shows favor and kindness, to those of us who love Him and obey Him. He also extends these blessings to our descendants (Exodus 20:6).

Among the ways in which He blesses people who love Him is that He:

> *"We have a building of God, a house not made with hands, eternal in the heavens."*
> **2 Corinthians 5:1 (KJV)**

- ❖ protects us from enemies (Psalm 23)
- ❖ defends us and fights our battles (2 Kings 19:32)
- ❖ comforts us (Isaiah 51:3)
- ❖ listens and responds to our prayers (Lamentations 3:56)
- ❖ knows and understands us (Psalm 44:21)
- ❖ will never leave or abandon us (Romans 8:35-39)
- ❖ provides for all our needs (Philipians 4:19).

41

Over the years, I've heard Christians tell how God miraculously sent someone — even a stranger — to meet a stressful economic need. I was somewhat skeptical of their testimonies about these special emissaries allegedly sent to them by God. Therefore, I was unprepared for the following experience.

As was our custom at Sunday morning services, my husband and I sat near the front of the church. One Sunday, after the sermon, our minister invited people to come to the altar to pray. This was always a delight to me. As I moved toward the aisle, I suddenly felt a strong urge to sit down. Not understanding why, I nevertheless, sat down again preparing to pray from my seat.

Just as I was bowing my head, I glanced at the aisle and saw Maryann hurrying to the altar. I closed my eyes, ready to pray. God startled me when He spoke to my spirit.

"Give Maryann fifty dollars."

I thought of all the other things that I could do with fifty dollars.

"But Lord," I said, "she doesn't look like she needs money. She'll probably get insulted, if I just walk up to her and give her money."

"Give her fifty dollars," came His reply.

"Okay." I sighed as I took out my checkbook and pen.

While the congregation prayed, I wrote a fifty-dollar check to Maryann.

When Maryann passed our pew on her way back from the altar, I noticed an uncharacteristically somber look on her face. After the service ended, I quickly turned around in search of her. She was standing several rows behind me. As I approached her, she greeted me warmly and embraced me as was the custom for members of our church.

Tense with nervousness about her possible reaction and with curiosity about why God sent me on this errand, I blurted out, "I don't know why, but the Lord told me to give you this." I shoved the check at her.

She took it, read it, and burst into tears. "Oh, thank the Lord!" she exclaimed. This normally reserved woman did not wipe away the joyful tears that cascaded down her face. "Thank you, Helen," she said embracing me vigorously. When she regained her composure, she explained that she lost her job several months ago. Her rent was overdue, and her landlord had given her until the next day to pay her rent or he would have her evicted. Friends and relatives had given Maryann what they could, but she lacked fifty dollars.

"I prayed all night," Maryann said. "I could not sleep. I begged the Lord to help me get fifty dollars. This," she said waving the check, "is the answer to my prayers. Thank you." She gave me a lingering embrace.

I left the church that morning in greater awe of God and how He sometimes works. He cured my skepticism by using me as a "special emissary" to bless Maryann.

Love, Suffering, and the Problem of Evil

As you anticipate the blessings that come from a love relationship with God through His Son, Jesus Christ, take note that God does not promise that we will never have financial or health problems, nor that the people we love will love us in return. No, He does not promise us a stress-free life.

In fact, our everyday lives can sometimes feel like battles between forces of wholeness and forces of destruction.

Seeing the pain, suffering, and evil in this world, some people have genuine difficulty in reconciling this harsh reality with belief in a loving, all-powerful God. We might wonder why a loving God would permit so much suffering to exist. Some of us might assert that if we were God, we would not run the universe in such a manner. Yet we need to remember the Scripture:

> "For my thoughts are not your thoughts, neither are your ways my ways, declares the Lord. For as the heavens are higher than the earth, so are my ways higher than your ways and my thoughts than your thoughts."
>
> **Isaiah 55:8-9**

God, in His infinite wisdom, has given us the freedom to love or reject Him, to do good or evil. We must face the reality that some people choose to use their freedom to inflict evil on others.

Our faith in God does not exempt us from suffering. In fact, some suffering is useful and can become the basis of our spiritual and emotional development. Sometimes, our own pain and suffering give us insight and compassion that we would not otherwise ever develop. Welcoming God's love and accepting His gift of Jesus Christ means that we can then count upon Him to be with us in the midst of our reality, however painful it is.

"...Count it all joy when you fall into various trials, knowing that the testing of your faith produces patience."

James 1:2-3 (NKJV)

Because of the love relationship we have with Him, God gives us the grace to deal with pain, suffering, and tragedy (1

44

Corinthians 10:13). Through the empowerment of His Holy Spirit, we become enabled to do and to bear far more than we ever could on our own human power. In my own life, I have experienced the reality of the Scripture that declares:

"He gives power to the weak, and to those who have no might He increases strength."

Isaiah 40:29 (NKJV)

"And we know that all things work together for good to those who love God and are called according to his purpose."

Romans 8:28 (NKJV)

Now whenever I go through pain and suffering, I remember that God is with me, and that He comforts and guides me. I also remember how God made past painful experiences help me to grow in faith , patience, compassion and wisdom. The insight I gain from my pain enriches the advice and counsel I am able to give to clients, family and friends. My suffering ultimately benefited other people as well as myself. I cannot honestly say that I welcome pain and suffering. I do not. But because I accept God's gifts of love, I am not as fearful of them nor as stressed about pain and suffering as I used to be.

"Blessed is the man who trusts in the Lord, And Whose hope is the Lord. For he shall be like a tree planted by the waters, Which spreads out its roots by the river, And will not fear when heat comes; But its leaf will be green, And will not be anxious in the year of drought, Nor will cease from yielding fruit."

Jeremiah 17:7-8 (NKJV)

REMEMBER

1. Regularly take time to enjoy God's gift of natural stress-relievers.

2. Accept Jesus Christ as Lord of your life. This is God's Supreme gift of love.

You and I are so much better equipped to deal with whatever life brings, if we have strong love relationships with God. Even if we welcome His love, some of us are not sure how to love God in return. We might rightly surmise that our love for Him is suppose to surpass our love for anyone or anything. But how on earth can we love God like that?

Principle 3
LOVE GOD

"You shall love the Lord, your God with all your heart, with all your soul and with all your mind."

Matthew 22:37

God, who is Love, seeks a loving response from us. Scripture exhorts us to love God passionately, with our whole selves (Deuteronomy 6:5; Matthew 22:37). It is this kind of passionate love of God that has, for more than two thousand years, sustained believers in the midst of horrendous experiences.

Love God With All Your Heart

This means to love God with complete sincerity and devotion. When we love like this, we willingly and eagerly attach ourselves to Him and take great pleasure in doing so. In short, we are on fire with love for Him. To develop a passionate love for God:

1. Read the Bible

The *Bible*, the Word of God, teaches us about Him, what He has done, and what He is doing for those who love Him. It helps us to learn how what He wants of us fits into His eternal plans. We also learn about the temporal and eternal rewards of obeying Him. Study

"All Scripture is given by inspiration of God and is profitable for doctrine, for reproof, for correction, for instruction in righteousness"

2 Timothy 3:16 (NKJV)

the *Bible* daily (Acts 17:11). Read one of the contemporary English translations, such as *The Living Bible*, the *New American Standard*, the *Amplified* or the *New King James Bible*. Use a study guide, such as *Bible Pathway*, which takes you through the entire Bible in one year. For brief daily study and meditation, I highly recommend, *Our Daily Bread*, distributed by RBC Ministries. (See the Appendix for the addresses of both publications.) There are several computer based Bible study aids. Among them are *Biblesoft's PC Study Bible for Windows* and *The Complete Multimedia Bible*. Both come in CD-ROM versions. *The Multimedia Bible* offers you an interactive way to experience the King James Version of the Bible.

2. Worship God daily

Periodically, throughout the day, praise Him. Express your adoration and reverence for who He is. Your individual celebrations of God will lift your emotions in ways that will astound you. At least once a week worship with others who love the Lord. Attend a church where the preaching and teachings are based upon the Bible. Participate in Bible studies with other believers. Their insights and experiences can enrich your understanding of who

"Bless the Lord, O my soul; and all that is within me, bless His holy name. Bless the Lord, O my soul; and forget not all his benefits."

Psalms 103:1-2 (NKJV)

God is and how He works on our behalf. The more that you learn about our loving God, the more deeply you will love Him. The further you advance in your studies, the more you will learn to apply biblical principles to your life. As a consequence, you will then be empowered to handle, and in some instances prevent, stress from even occurring.

3. Sing to the Lord

The *Bible* specifically exhorts us to sing to the Lord (Exodus15: 21; Psalms 68:4; Jeremiah 20:13; Ephesians 5:19; Colossians 3:16; James 5:13).

We increase our love for God and reduce our stress when we sing songs like *"What A Mighty God We Serve"* or *"A Mighty Fortress is our God"*. These kinds of songs:

❖ Give praise and honor to God. That pleases Him and lifts our spirits.

❖ Remind us of God's qualities, i.e., power, mercy, love, wisdom, delight in protecting, and giving good things to His children, etc.

> *"Therefore I will give thanks to you, O Lord ...And sing praises to Your name."*
>
> 2 Samuel 22:50 (NKJV)

❖ Are love songs to God. When we express our love for God in song, we often find that the melody helps to communicate our deeply felt emotions more powerfully than words can alone.

Some Christians sing to God "in tongues,"i.e., glossalalia, relying upon the Holy Spirit to express the deepest feelings of their hearts. Some sing this way everyday and find that it gives them inner strength to effectively deal with whatever life brings.

My mother often sang to the Lord. Her songs to God are among the most memorable recollections of my childhood. I recall that during times when she was anguishing about my two teenage brothers, who were members of a fighting street gang, she would go into the kitchen and start cleaning her already clean cabinets. From my room, I could hear her contralto voice in concert for God. When my brothers were out too late, she'd sing:

"Precious Lord, take my hand.
Lead me on, Let me stand.
I am tired. I am weak. I am worn.
Through the storm, through the night Lead me on to the light.
Take my hand, Precious Lord, lead me on."

One night after a rival gang shot and killed our neighbor's son, my brothers were, again, out past their curfew. The terror in my mother's voice lessened only after hours of singing songs like, *"Nobody knows the trouble I've seen. Nobody knows but Jesus,"* or *"Pass me not, O Gentile Savior, Hear my humble cry."* As she felt God comforting her, she sang, *"Blessed Assurance, Jesus is mine."* My mother's concert for God ended only after my brothers finally returned home safely. Late at night, my mother's songs of praise would echo through our apartment. I fell asleep hearing Mama sing, *"What a friend we have in Jesus."*

"I waited patiently for The Lord; And He inclined to me, And heard my cry. He also brought me up out of a horrible pit, Out of miry clay, And set my feet upon a rock, And established my steps. He has put a new song in my mouth—Praise to our God..."

Psalms 40:1-3 (NKJV)

As an adult I, too, have found that my love for God grows whenever I sing love songs to Him, especially when singing with other believers. Passion for God gives me confidence that no matter what stress I encounter "With God, nothing will be impossible" (Luke 1:37).

Love God With All Your Soul

This means loving God with all of your will—that spiritual part of you that determines your personality and behavior. When you love God with all your soul, you gladly surrender to Him. Like Jesus, you can sincerely say, "Not my will, but Yours be done" (Luke 22:42). Then you eagerly cooperate with the development of Godly qualities in your personality. As children of God, we delight in resembling Him.

Encourage the development of this Godly transformation of your personality.

Trust God

Trust is another word for faith. We all know, from our human relationships, that trust is essential for a sound relationship. Trust, or faith in God's integrity, is all the more important in our relationship with Him. *"For without faith, it is impossible to please God"* (Hebrews 11:6). The health of your spiritual journey depends upon deciding to believe what God promised and trust His integrity to do it. This confident expectation puts you in a position to receive peace of mind, even in frightening situations. For example:

Fran was sound asleep when it happened. The sharp violent movements shook her awake.

"Mommie!" her son screamed from his room. In the darkness, Fran scrambled out of bed. Her room convulsed. She heard dishes, glasses, and books crashing to the floor.

"Mommie!"

"I'm coming," she shouted, stumbling towards his room as the house shook and swayed. Holding onto the walls, which themselves trembled, she made her way to her hysterical child.

"Here I am, Baby," she said, trying to sound calmer than she felt. Grasping her five-year old to her, she explained, "Its an earthquake." As she hastily moved the two of them to the doorframe for protection, her son's toy fire truck burst from the closet and struck his foot. The child screamed.

Suddenly the earth was silent and still. With nerves taunt and eyes trying in vain to see in the darkness, they heard tenants in adjoining apartments shouting and frantically moving around. Again the earth rumbled and shook. They heard wrenching, cracking sounds.

"Mommie!" her son screamed again, clinging desperately to his only parent.

"Jesus, help us! Lord, protect us!" Fran prayed. Embracing her crying child, she cried out for God's help. Her heart pounded in alarm. But she continued to pray. After awhile she was certain that the Lord heard her and she grew calmer.

After the quakes stopped, Fran carefully led her son back to bed. She lay down beside him, whispering, "Hush, Baby. Everything's gonna be all right." Soon they fell asleep.

This pre-dawn earthquake of January 17, 1994 was one of the worst in the history of Los Angeles, California. President George Bush, Sr. declared it a national emergency. Like hundreds of other buildings, the apartment house in which Fran lived shifted off its foundation. It was later declared uninhabitable.

The city was in turmoil. Thousands of people fled California. Many of those who stayed were traumatized. Children and adults had nightmares and were obsessed with memories of the upheaval in their lives. For months after the quake, the earth repeatedly shook with aftershocks.

Hundreds of families who were displaced from their homes had to sleep in public parks and makeshift shelters.

In the midst of the commotion of the city, Fran felt God's presence. Friends from her church opened their homes to her and her son. Fran kept on praying. Her employer allowed her to take time off from work to look for safe and affordable housing. As she went about the arduous tasks of salvaging what she could of their meager possessions, Fran continued praying and trusting God. He blessed her with a peace "that passes all understanding" (Philipians 4:7). Seeing her calmness soothed her child's jangled nerves. God blessed them with the people, money, and resources they needed to re-establish their lives.

> *"Now faith is the substance of things hoped for, the evidence of things not seen."*
> **Hebrews 11:1 (NKJV)**

Fran's faith in God and her commitment to Him, enabled her to manage the multiple stressors that literally shook her world that day and for months after.

Love God with All Your Mind

Loving God with all our minds means that you and I love Him with all our intellects, abilities to reason, imaginations, and our memories.

Intellect and Reasoning

When we love Him with our intellect, we are thirsty to learn as much about God as we can. Our finite minds can never fully understand Him. Nevertheless, we strive to understand as much as we can of His ways, His will, and His character. In practical terms this means:

1. We <u>study</u>, not merely read the Bible. Often this requires that we attend Bible study classes, go to a Bible college or attend a seminary.

    We eagerly seek to learn from anointed and gifted teachers who are steeped in biblical knowledge and whose lives reflect their deep love of God.

2. We use our intellects and abilities to reason to search out the meaning of Scripture and its implications for how we should live our lives and manage our stresses.

3. We actively search for opportunities to hear the sermons of anointed preachers who can help us to better understand the Christian way of life.

"O the depth of the riches both of the wisdom and knowledge of God! How unsearchable are His judgments, and His ways past finding out!"

Romans 11:33 (NKJV)

"Be ready always to give an answer to every man that asketh you a reason of the hope that is in you."

1 Peter 3:15 (KJV)

"Cast thy burdens upon the Lord, and He shall sustain thee; He shall never suffer the righteous to be moved."

Psalm 55:22 (KJV)

Imagination

You can exercise your imagination and creativity to express your love for God. The process of creativity can be a wonderful way to relieve stress as it engrosses your attention.

Even seeing or hearing the works that others created to honor God can increase your love for Him and your ability to reduces stress. At one time, some of us have been relaxed, emotionally transported, or inspired by the creative works of Christians like Johann Sebastian Bach

"So then faith comes by hearing and hearing by the word of God."

Romans 10:17 (NKJV)

and Michaelangelo. When you use your imagination to give honor to God, the level of your skill is not as important as your intent to use your imagination to express your love for God.

Try some of the following:

❖ Write a poem, an essay, a sermon, a novel, a play, a devotional, a song, or a hymn about God.

❖ Paint, sculpt, crochet, knit, make a collage, embroider or do some other creative handiwork that gives praises to God.

❖ Dance unto the Lord, as David did. (2 Samuel 6:14)

❖ Act in a church play, direct one, or help design and make the scenery or costumes.

> *"Praise the Lord!*
> *Sing to the Lord a*
> *new song, And*
> *His praise in the*
> *assembly of*
> *saints.... Let them*
> *praise His name*
> *with the dance;*
> *Let them sing*
> *praises to Him*
> *with the timbrel*
> *and harp."*
> **Psalm 149:1-3**
> **(NKJV)**

❖ Volunteer work can also put one's stress into perspective, i.e., the man who's sorry for himself because he has no shoes and meets the man with no feet. Also, helping others work through their problems can help you see solutions in your own parallel stressors.

Memory

You love God with your memory when you remember Him every day. When you actively recall how good God is to you, you

> *"From the*
> *rising of the*
> *sun until the*
> *going down of*
> *the same the*
> *Lord's Name is*
> *to be praised."*
> **Psalms 113.3**
> **(NKJV)**

will feel empowered to better deal with your life, especially your stressors.

Do the following:

1. Tell people about God and how He blesses you. Be specific. The more often you tell people, the more you will remember and thereby more fully love God. As a consequence, your love connection with God is strengthened, and He will help you with whatever you encounter in life.

2. In your journal write a list showing how God has blessed you. Think of "small" as well as "large" blessings. Add to your **List of Blessings** frequently.

3. Memorize Scripture. Be like the psalmist who declared, *"Thy word will I hide in my heart so that I may not sin against thee."* (Psalm 119:11). Start by memorizing:

    ❖ Psalm 23

    ❖ Genesis 1:1

    ❖ John 3:16

    ❖ Joshua 1:8

    ❖ Jeremiah 29:11

    ❖ Matthew 22:37

As humans, none of us can ever become perfect in our passionate love of God. As with everything else God asks us

"How excellent is thy lovingkindness O God! Therefore the children of men put their trust under the shadow of thy wings."

Psalm 36:7 (KJV)

"The grass withers, the flower fades, but the Word of our God stands forever."

Isaiah 40:8 (NKJV)

"Teach me thy way, O Lord; I will walk in thy truth."

Psalm 86:11 (KJV)

"Blessed be the Lord, who daily loadeth us with benefits, even the God of our salvation."

Psalm 68:19 (KJV)

to do, He is willing to empower us to obey Him through His Holy Spirit (John 14:15-17).

Let God's Holy Spirit Empower You

The Holy Ghost (Spirit) empowers us by:

"You shall know the truth and the truth will set you free."

John 8:32 (NKJV)

◆ **Revealing** the truth to us (John 14:17, 26; 1 Corinthians 2:13). This helps us with stress caused by our not knowing the truth about something that concerns us. When we pray and listen for God's answer, we can experience the calmness that comes from the assurance that, in His time, God will reveal to us the truth of the matter.

◆ **Comforting** us (Acts 9:31; John 14:16). When we are stressed by threats and disappointments, we can be comforted by God's Holy Spirit. When I went through times of crisis, I'd ask, from the depth of my heart, for God to comfort me. Every single time, He soothed and comforted me through His Holy Spirit. In time, I learned not to grieve so deeply, because I knew He was with me.

◆ **Guiding** (John 16:13; Psalm 25:9). The decisions we make are crucial in determining the level of stress we will have in life. Any poor choices we make today are down payments on tomorrow's problems. However, even when horrendous things happen to us, we still have a choice about how we will respond to them. Through His Holy Spirit, God helps us to make wise choices.

"I will instruct and Teach you in the way you should go; I will guide you with My eye."

Psalm 32:8 (NKJV)

◆ **Transforming** our character (2 Corinthians 3:18). As we continually submit our souls to God, our personalities become more like His son, Jesus (1 John 3). We become more loving, joyful, peaceful, patient, kind, good, faithful, gentle and self-disciplined people (Galatians 5:22-23).

"The Spirit itself beareth witness with our spirit that we are the children of God."
Romans 8:16 (KJV)

We avoid, reduce, or manage our stress better when we choose to deal with potential or actual stressors with patience, self-control, and loyalty to God, to those we love, and to ourselves.

The process of learning how to love God with all our hearts, all our souls, and all our minds is the most important thing we can do in life.

God already loves you and me. We can become *"more than conquerors"* (Romans 8:37) of the stressors in our lives as we cooperate with God in learning to truly love Him.

"I will strengthen thee; yea, I will help thee; yea, I will uphold thee with the right hand of my righteousness."
Isaiah 41:10 (KJV)

REMEMBER

1. God's stress management plans is built upon our having a fervent love relationship with Him

2. He already loves you unconditionally

3. Grow to love Him fervently by doing the following every day:

- ❖ Study the Bible
- ❖ Praise and worship Him
- ❖ Pray and sing in your heart to Him
- ❖ Trust Him
- ❖ Let your thoughts and imagination be filled with Him.
- ❖ Memorize scripture
- ❖ Let the Holy Spirit guide you in your every day life.

We prove that we really love God when we consistenly obey Him.

Principle 4
OBEY GOD

"If you love me, keep my commandments."
John 14:15 (NIV)

We bring a host of needless problems and stresses upon ourselves when we disobey God.

We can see this more clearly when we consider the consequences of disobedience i.e., sin. We can sin by omission, that is, we fail to do what God wants us to do. Or we can sin by commission, which is doing what God expressly tells us not to do. To illustrate how we can needlessly bring stress into our lives, let us consider the consequences of committing the "Seven Deadly Sins." They are pride, greed, gluttony, envy, lust, wrath, and sloth.

Pride (Psalms 101:5; Proverbs 6:17)
Pride is the chief among sins. If we are prideful, we think more highly of ourselves than is realistically warranted.

Pride is often the underlying attitude that leads us to ignore or deliberately choose to defy God. It was Satan's pride that led him to rebel against God. And he appealed to Eve's pride to motivate her to disobey God (Genesis 3:1-6). Pride deludes us into

"Pride goes before destruction, And a haughty spirit before a fall"
Proverbs 16:18 (NKJV)

thinking that we know better than God how we should live our lives.

When we are prideful, we tend to believe that we are better than other people. Viewing them through pride-tainted lenses, we tend to be judgmental and critical of them.

Such arrogance on our part makes other people angry, and alienates us from them, as well as from God.

For example:

Winston is a very successful businessman in a highly competitive industry. He takes great pride in his accomplishments and insists that others acknowledge his superiority. As a consequence, he has little tolerance when others hold opinions different from his own, and he uses sarcasm and his biting wit to intimidate them. At dinner parties, he monopolizes the conversations and insults other guests. Few people are willing to socialize with him.

The love his wife once felt for him has cooled considerably. She complains that his overbearing pride makes him insensitive to her need to be valued and respected. She is considering a divorce. Winston is extremely upset. He says that he loves his wife and does not want to lose her. She, however, wonders how much of his declaration of love for her is really related to the damage a divorce will bring to his ego and to his public image.

Even though Winston is a prominent leader in his church and regularly contributes his tithes and offerings, his personal relationship with God is characterized more by the pride that he takes in following the rules of the Bible, than by a passionate love of God. As a consequence, his pride interferes with the help God is willing to give him in managing stress and other aspects of his life.

Gluttony (Deuteronomy 21:20; Proverbs 23:21; Matthew 11:19)

Gluttony is the sin of excessive eating. It leads people to abuse their bodies through obesity and its attendant health problems. This displeases God, because our bodies are the temples of His Spirit (1 Corinthians 3:16-17). Considering the serious damage that gluttony can do to the body, one can say that the sin of gluttony is a kind of desecration of God's temple. Another penalty of gluttony can be stress. For example:

Hank has been overweight since adolescence. Today, he weighs over 300 pounds. He continuously thinks about food. Consequently at work, he has difficulty concentrating on his job. His happy-go-lucky demeanor barely hides his deep shame about the way that he looks. Women are turned off by his appearance, and men ridicule him. Hank's doctor warns him that being overweight worsens his hypertension and increases his risks of a stroke and of heart disease. Hank feels unable to curb his eating. Whenever he thinks about his poor health and miserable social life, Hank gets anxious and depressed. He eats to feel better — at least temporarily.

Gluttony is also the sin of excessive consumption of alcohol. Alcoholics and other problem drinkers invite stress into their own lives as well as the lives of family, friends, and others. Hospitals are filled with casualties of automobile accidents caused by drunk drivers. Adults and children who once lived active, productive lives have become quadriplegics, are comatose, or are dead as a result of someone's gluttonous use of alcohol.

Although the Bible does not specifically mention marijuana, heroin, cocaine, PCP, and other narcotics, I believe that their use and abuse is another form of gluttony. Like alcohol, these substances befuddle our minds and damage our bodies. If we use narcotics, we will progressively turn the control of our lives over to these substances instead of to God. Sooner or later, this form of gluttony will bring great spiritual, emotional, financial, and social stresses into our lives.

> *"For the drunkard and the glutton will come to poverty. And drowsiness will clothe a man with rags."*
> **Proverbs 23:21 (NKJV)**

Greed (Proverbs 21:26; 1 Timothy 3:3 & 8)

Although greed, like gluttony, is a sin of excess, greed is not restricted to food, alcohol, and drugs. Greed can be an excessive desire for obtaining anything. We can be greedy for money, possessions, attention, power, or excitement, and the like. For instance:

> *"He who is greedy for gain, troubles his own house..."*
> **Proverbs 15:27 (NKJV)**

Nancy has closets full of clothing she bought and has never worn. She can barely pass a store without going in to "browse" and coming out with shoes, handbags, and other items she does not need. She loves the attention, admiration, and sometimes envy others show her because of her stylish fashions. Nevertheless, Nancy is chronically anxious and has frequent stomach pains. She wakes up during the night, worrying about her mounting credit card debts.

The objects of our greed tend to occupy the place in our lives that should be reserved for God. We tend to idolize the things about which we are greedy and give them power over how we live our lives.

Greed is often associated with other vices. To obtain the objects of their excessive desire, some people gamble, swindle, embezzle, lie, deceive, manipulate, or even kill. We frequently read about grasping bankers, corporate executives, politicians, and others who embezzled money to support lavish life-styles. By giving into greed and its associated sins, they inflicted upon themselves the stresses inherent in ruined reputations, destroyed family lives, and in the bankruptcies of people who trusted them.

The Bible specifically warns against the stresses that result from greediness for money.

> *"But those who desire to be rich fall into temptation and a snare and into many foolish and harmful lusts which drown men in destruction and perdition. For the love of money is a root of all kinds of evil, for which some have strayed from the faith in their greediness and pierced themselves through with many sorrows."*

1 Timothy 6:6-11 (NKJV)

Envy (Proverbs 27:4; Romans 1:29)

Envy is the sin of covetousness and jealousy. When we envy others we not only want what they have, but often resent them for having it. For example:

> *Eva has frequent bouts of envy. Almost any woman can be the focus of her covetousness and spite. She is rarely happy about other people's good fortune. In fact, her fragile self-esteem is threatened when others have what she does not. When her sister received a ruby ring from her boyfriend, Eva got into an argument with her own boyfriend, demanding that he buy her an expensive ring, preferable one more costly than her sister's. Eva's envy and*

competitiveness keeps her tense and depressed and strains her relationships with others.

> "For where envy and self seeking exist, Confusion and every evil thing is there."
>
> James 3:16 (NKJV)

Envy also strains our love relationships with God. When we envy, we tend to disparage what He has already given us, thereby revealing an ungrateful heart. Envy of the talents and abilities of others sometimes keeps us from appreciating, and therefore developing, the unique gifts and abilities with which God has blessed us. Envy stresses us with discontent and dampens our passions for God.

Sloth (James 18:9; Proverbs 12:24 & 27; Hebrews 6:12)

Sloth is the sin of laziness. We don't want to work or exert ourselves. We are apathetic, and especially unconcerned about the things that matter to God. Slothful people waste their talents, abilities, and opportunities. Consequently, when we are slothful, we are poor stewards of the resources God gives us for the work of His kingdom and for our enjoyment of life. For instance:

Ray is an exceptionally bright and gifted writer. He has wonderfully creative ideas for novels and screenplays. He started several of them, but finished only one short story. When his friends visit him, he moves piles of clothes and newspapers from the sofa so that they can sit down. He searches for cups among the crusty dishes in his kitchen sink to wash them so that he can offer his guests some coffee. As they talk about his friends' accomplishments, Ray feels both inspired and envious. Familiar feelings of shame and frustration nag him about his own lack of productivity and success. After awhile, he hears himself criticizing and belittling his friends. They soon leave.

After they leave, Ray is beset with guilt for what he said. He also feels guilty about wasting his talents. He thinks that he ought to finish writing the screenplay he began last month. He gets up to go to his word processor. On the way, he notices the TV guide and picks it up. After leafing through it, he decides to watch a favorite show, before writing. Several hours later, he thinks that it is too late to write and he needs to go to bed. He tells himself that he will write tomorrow.

Sloth corrodes the gifts and abilities, which God gives us. When we give into it, we can become lazy about praying, reading the Bible, going to church, doing good for others, and taking proper care of ourselves. These attitudes and behaviors weaken our passion for God. They also make us more vulnerable to the stresses that result from procrastination and "not taking care of business."

Wrath (Psalms 37:8; Romans 2:8; Ephesians 4:31)
Wrath is the sin of deep and excessive anger. A person who has a quick temper and is easily offended is guilty of wrath. A wrathful person holds grudges and seeks to punish others or to get revenge. In extreme cases, wrath consumes the person. For example:

When people first met Olga, they were impressed with her pretty smile. But after awhile, they began to feel uncomfortable. They noticed that Olga was easily angered. She wouldn't say why she was upset. She just became cold and distant. The few people who did not give up trying to get her to smile again found that they had "to walk on egg shells" to get along with her. During the many periods when no one called or visited her, Olga re-examined the resentments she collected over the years. Last year,Olga shot herself to death. Her suicide devastated her son who was one of the people with whom she was most angry.

In their excessive rage, wrathful people say and do cruel things, often wrecking havoc on themselves and others. We have all been horrified at the reports of wrathful employees going on shooting sprees, killing their bosses and co-workers. Enraged, angry husbands slap, kick, and beat up their wives and children and thereby cause repeated, if not chronic stress for themselves and their families.

Except for righteous anger against sin (not the sinner), our rage evicts any passion we may have for God. When we are wrathful, we are not loving of God, other people, nor ourselves. When we are wrathful, we, in effect, hate our way into stress.

> *"So then...let everyone be swift to hear, slow to speak, slow to wrath;for the wrath of man does not produce the righteousness of God."*
>
> **James 1:19-20 (NKJV)**

Lust (Proverbs 6:23-29; Matthew 5:28; Romans 1:27; 2 Peter 2:10)

Lust is the sin of inordinate desire to gratify bodily appetites, especially unrestrained sexual gratification. A lustful person indulges in one or more of the sexual behaviors specifically condemned by Scripture. These sins are:

❖ **fornication**, i.e., sexual intercourse between an unmarried male and female
(Romans 1:29; 1 Corinthians 6:18).

❖ **adultery**, i.e., at least one of the sexual partners is married to someone else
(Exodus 20:14; Galatians 5:19).

67

❖ **homosexuality**, i.e., sexual relations between people of the same gender (Leviticus 18:22, 20:13; Romans 1:24-27).

❖ **bestiality**, i.e., sexual relations with an animal (Leviticus 18:23).

❖ **incest**, i.e., unlawful sexual relations with relatives (Leviticus 18:6-18).

It has become commonplace in our society for people to become sexually intimate as a "normal" part of dating. I have counseled innumerable people who were stressed by guilt for their sexual activities or by the shame they felt about the multiple partners they've had over the years in their search for the "right mate." Both women and men have felt a deeper sense of abandonment and betrayal when people with whom they had been sexually intimate ended the relationships.

Among the many other stressors that are direct outcomes of sexual sins are unwanted pregnancies, abortions, herpes, HIV, AIDS, other sexually transmitted diseases, divorces and deaths.

"To set the mind on flesh is death, but to set the mind on the Spirit is life and peace"

Romans 8:6 (RSV)

Some lustful people don't actually do any of the above, but spend a lot of time fantasizing about doing them. In Jesus's view the person who lusts in his mind and imagination is guilty of sin (Matthew 5:28). For instance:

Kenneth loves to watch pornography. He tries to get his wife to watch the videos with him. She refuses because she found that it cheapens their sex life. Mimicking the videos robbed their sexual relations of romance and emotional intimacy. So Kenneth often watches pornography alone and masturbates. Some nights after viewing these videos, Kenneth goes to bed fully aroused. He barely caresses his wife before he begins coitus with her. Feeling used, she often cries herself to sleep. Recently, she has begun to refuse to have sexual relations with him. Their fights have gotten worse. There is a great deal of tension in their marriage. Reacting to the family stress, their seven-year-old son has begun rebelling in school.

The spiritual side of us is continually at war with the carnal side of our nature (Romans 8:1-8). We best love God when we use our will and His help to control our carnal appetites. For some of us, this may be more difficult than for others. Some people have very strong libido or sexual urges. Whether or not you or I have such strong urges, our loving God has established guidelines for how to manage them so that they enhance rather than damage our lives. In our passionate responses to God's love, we eagerly surrender our bodily passions to His will and control.

This discussion of the Seven Deadly Sins was not meant to imply that these are the only sins that we can commit. Nor are they the only ones that can bring us stress. The discussion was only to illustrate how damaging sin is to us. When we love God passionately, we yield our wills to Him and cooperate with His plans for our well being.

REMEMBER

Always be alert to how sin may contribute to your stress. Write the answers to the following in your journal.

1. What part does pride play in your stress experience?
    a) About what do you tend to feel insulted?
    b) How much of your stress is related to frustration that you cannot have your way?
    c) Has God forgiven you for something that you have not forgiven yourself?

2. What part of your stress is the result of envy?
    a) Are there people whom you envy because of what they have or some characteristic they possess?
    b) Do you resent that God has apparently blessed someone else with what you want and think you do not have?

3. What part of your stress is the result of your lust?
    a) Which of the sexual expressions prohibited by Scripture have you committed in body or mind?
    b) What are the consequences to you and/or to those you love?

4. What part of your stress is related to greed?
    a) For what do you have an inordinately intense desire?
    b) What are the spiritual, emotional, physical, financial, and/or social costs of this intense yearning?

5. What part of your stress is related to gluttony?
    What are the physical, financial, emotional, social, and spiritual costs to you?

6. What part does wrath play in your stress experience?
    a) Are you easily irritated?

b) Do you lose control and harm others, verbally, physically or in some other way?

7. What part does sloth play in your stress experience?

   How has laziness or procrastination contributed to your stress?

8. How has your failure to do something, which the Scriptures specifically tell us to do contributing to your stress? i.e., show kindness to others; forgive others; give to those in need; encourage others, etc.

Prayerfully decide what you will do to remove these spiritual causes of stress in your life. Ask God to help you. Consider whether you also need the help of a counselor or others who love God, to help you live a more stress-resistant life.

Principle 5
ALWAYS PRAY

"Pray without ceasing."
1 Thessalonians 5:17 (NKJV)

If you and I are to have strong love relationships with God, it is essential that we pray. We must talk to and listen to Him continually. Jesus taught that we *"ought always to pray"* (Luke 18:17).

> *"They shall call on my Name, and I will hear them; I will say, It is my people; and they shall say, The Lord is my God."*
> **Zechariah 13:9 (KJV)**

Our prayers can be spontaneous expressions like **"Thank you Lord for this beautiful day."** Or like Father Murray Bodo, our simple prayers can express a concern. **"Lord, let me remember that every word I speak reflects my experience of you. Teach me the words that live."**[1]

Sometimes it is hard for us to find the words that accurately express what we feel. In those instances, prayers composed by others can be very helpful. Some of these composed or liturgical prayers said during Christian worship

---

1   Bodo, Murray, O.F.M. ,Tale of St. Francis Ancient Stories for Contemporary Living (New York: Doubleday, 1988)

services help us focus on God's agenda and then we decide to make our own. For example, you may find that words of the prayer of St Francis of Assisi accurately expresses what you want to say to God.

"Lord, make me an instrument of your peace.
Where there is hatred, let me sow love;
Where there is injury, pardon;
Where there is doubt, faith;
Where there is despair, hope;
Where there is darkness, light;
And where there is sadness, joy.
O Divine Master,
Grant that I may not so much seek to
be consoled as to console,
To be understood as to understand,
To be loved as to love;
For it is in giving that we receive;
It is in pardoning that we are pardoned;
And it is in dying that we are born to eternal life"[2]

"Forgive us our trespasses as we forgive those who trespass against us."
Matthew 6:12 (KJV)

I believe that our prayer life should be balanced with the prayers we compose — however clumsy they may be — and with time-tested liturgical prayers. Our spontaneous prayers increase our intimacy with God the Father. On the other hand, liturgical prayers help us to avoid the danger of forgetting that God is Sovereign and the Creator and Ruler of the universe. The stateliness and formality of liturgical prayers help us to remember His awesomeness and the profound respect we owe Him.

2   Ibid. 81

In our love relationship with God we will pray a variety of spontaneous and liturgical prayers. Among them are prayers of:

"Lord teach us to pray...."
Luke 11:1 (KJV)

Praise and Adoration

These are prayers that focus on the goodness of God and on His unique qualities. In these prayers we esteem God above all things. We acknowledge that His power is awesome and we pay homage to His infinite wisdom.

"Great is the Lord and greatly to be praised."
1 Chronicles 16:25 (KJV)

As we praise God for who He is, we are reminded of the infinite spiritual resources available to us for avoiding, reducing, and managing stress.

"I will bless the Lord at all times; His praises shall continually be in my mouth."
Psalm 34:1 (KJV)

Thanksgiving

Closely related to prayers of adoration and praise are prayers in which we thank God for who He is, what He has done in the past, what He is doing in the present, and what He will do in the future. Scripture tells us:

"In everything give thanks, for this is the will of God in Christ Jesus for you."
1 Thessalonians 5:18 (NIV)

"God is my salvation; I will trust and not be afraid; for the Lord Jehovah is my strength and my song."
Isaiah 12:2 (KJV)

On one level this seems to mean that no matter how stressful our situation, we can find something for which to thank God. For example, you may have a belligerent boss, and you are distressed by the hostile way that he treats you. Nevertheless, you can thank God for having a job.

On a more radical level, the Bible says that you and I should thank God *for* all things. Ephesians 5:20 says:

"...always giving thanks to God the Father for everything, in the name of our Lord Jesus Christ."

Using the above example, you should also thank God *for* your belligerent boss and the hostile way that he treats you. Wow! As unnatural as that seems, I can tell you that if you do, you can become considerably less distressed. My favorite account of this principle at work is one told by the evangelist, Corrie ten Boom.

Corrie and her sister Betsie were in Ravensbruck, a Nazi concentration camp. They had just arrived at this terrible prison and Corrie was worried about what awaited them. She was also extremely annoyed by the hordes of lice in their dormitory. Corrie's sister Betsie said, "Let's pray and thank God."

"Be not afraid neither be thou dismayed, for the Lord thy God is with thee whithersoever thou goest."

Joshua 1:9 (KJV)

*Corrie welcomed the suggestion that they pray. She prayed aloud, asking God to help them in their circumstances. When she finished praying, Betsie reminded her that she had not thanked God *for* their circumstances, including the lice, which were biting them even as she spoke. Fighting her skepticism about this, Corrie decided to obey God's Word. She bowed her head in prayer and thanked God for everything, including the lice.*

"When thou passest through the waters I will be with thee; and through the rivers, they shall not overflow thee."

Isaiah 43:2 (KJV)

Over the next few months, Corrie and Betsie held secret Bible studies in their prison dormitory. Corrie rejoiced as many of the women prisoners came to Christ. She was surprised that they had been able to conduct these forbidden Bible studies, unhindered by their prison guards. The lice continued to bite Corrie, but she was no longer stressed by them. One day, Corrie discovered the reason why she and Betsie were able to bring the Good News of Christ to so many prisoners. The Nazis who guarded their dormitory detested lice. Consequently, they avoided going into the dormitory. Those biting lice, for which Corrie had given God thanks, guarded her from the Nazis!

> *"I am with thee and will keep thee in all places whither thou goest."*
>
> **Genesis 28:15 (KJV)**

The circumstances of being imprisoned in a Nazi concentration camp were horrifying. Yet they continued to thank God. After the end of World War II, Corrie became an evangelist. She went around the world, speaking of Christ to millions of people in more than 60 countries on every continent.

Millions of people have been inspired by this woman whose inner strength developed as a result of saying prayers of thanksgiving to God *for* all things in *all* circumstances. Young and old people who heard her speak or read her books came to accept Christ as their Lord and Savior. As a result, their lives were transformed. In retrospect, Corrie, indeed, should have thanked God *for* her imprisonment and *for* the lice. It was her love relationship with God in such bleak circumstances that added such authenticity to her witness.

> *"Whatsoever is born of God overcometh the world; and this is the victory that overcometh the world, even our faith."*
>
> **1 John 5:4 (KJV)**

Whatever the circumstances of your life, heed the Scripture and thank God. Trust that He will, somehow, *"make*

all things work together for the good of those who love Him and are
called according to His purpose" Romans 8:28 (NKJ).

> *"It is good to give thanks to the Lord,*
> *And to sing praises to Your Name,*
> *O Most High;*
> *To declare Your lovingkindness in the morning,*
> *And Your faithfulness every night, ...*
> *For You, Lord, have made me*
> *glad through Your work;*
> *I will triumph in the works of Your hands."*
>
> **Psalm 92:1,2,4 (NKJ)**

Petition and Supplication

These are probably the types of prayers that we most often
pray. In prayers of petition, we ask God for something. In
prayers of supplication we pray from the bottom of our
hearts, i.e., we beg Him.

Unfortunately, some people have
great difficulty praying prayers in which
they ask for something for themselves. I've
heard people say that they don't bother God
with the "little things" they can handle

"If you ask any
thing in my
name, I will do
it."

John 14:14 (NKJ)

themselves. They only turn to God for the "big things." I
believe that this is a dangerous practice. The so-called "big
things" in our lives are often the outcomes of the "little
things" — the little decisions we made, the little words we
spoke, the little tasks we failed to do. When we seek God's
guidance and help with the "little everyday things," we will
have fewer big things to stress us.

Others who are reluctant to pray for themselves think that such prayers are selfish. But Jesus said that God, the Father *"delights in giving good things to His children"* (Matthew 7:11). You and I also need to remember that we are to love other people *as* we love ourselves. Since the quality of our self-love is important to the quality of our love of other people, I think that it is important that we regularly pray for ourselves as an expression of self-love. Otherwise, we unnecessarily deprive ourselves of the greatest resources in the universe for managing our lives and our stress.

> *"Trust in the Lord with all thine heart; and lean not unto thine own understanding In all thy ways acknowledge Him, and He shall direct thy paths."*
>
> **Proverbs 3:5-6 (KJV)**

Meeting God and learning what He wants of us is far more important than what we want of God. When we pray in this way, we often receive better than we ever would have dared to ask, on our own.

Intercession

Intercessory prayers are those we pray in behalf of others. This is an important responsibility we have in our love relationship with God. When we intercede for others it reduces our stress in several ways. First, we are distracted from our own stress, as we focus on the needs of other people. Secondly, God is motivated to help or bless that person when we pray. Many times, the cause of our stress is worry about another person. When we pray for that person, we help to mobilize all the resources of heaven for that person's benefit. For example:

> *Several years ago, I was in a counseling session with Emily, a fifty-six-year-old woman who had been living for eight*

years with Neal who was thirty-nine. Initially, Neal was a boarder in Emily's home. In time, they became lovers.

Eventually, Neal lost his job and occasionally earned money as a house painter and handyman. Emily became his provider. With his dependence upon her, he became increasingly possessive. Sometimes, to assert his control, he physically assaulted her.

Emily sought my help because she wanted to get out of this relationship. She and I worked together for several months. During that time, her self-esteem increased and she became more assertive with Neal. As a Christian, Emily knew that her sexual relationship with Neal was outside of God's will. She asserted herself with Neal and ended their fornication. She also successfully stood up to him, and he stopped hitting her. Emily became more self-confident and felt ready to make a complete break with Neal.

"I told Neal that I don't want us to live together anymore," Emily told me.

"How did he take that news?" I asked.

Emily pulled a white tissue from her purse. Twisting it, she said, "He got mad." She dabbed her forehead, "He's a devil," she concluded.

"Why do you think that he's a devil?"

"He said that if I left him, he would shoot me...I know that he has a gun. I've seen it," she said, dropping her head.

Looking up at me, Emily continued, "He said that he would come here and shoot you, too."

"The Lord will give strength unto His people; the Lord will bless his people with peace."
Psalm 29:11 (NKJ)

"Your father knoweth what things ye have need of, before you ask Him."
Matthew 6:8 (KJV)

"Before they call, I will answer; and while they are yet speaking, I will hear."
Isaiah 65:24 (KJV)

I became frightened for our safety. My immediate response was to pray to God for protection. As I instinctively prayed silently, I felt led by God to pray aloud with Emily.

"The Lord is nigh unto all them that call upon Him."
Psalm 145:18 (KJV)

"Let's pray about this," I said.

"Okay," Emily said. She bowed her head.

"Holy Father," *I began,* **"You know that Neal has threatened to shoot us. Please protect us. Don't let any harm come to us."**

As I prayed, I felt God's peace. But I felt a prompting. I sensed that I was forgetting something. In my mind's eye, I saw Neal. For the first time, I felt a deep compassion for him. **"Father,"** *I continued,* **"You love Neal as much as you love Emily and me. Neal is frightened, Lord. He is hurting. Have mercy upon him... Guide us, Lord. Give us the wisdom we need to resolve this situation so that there is no violence. Give us the love we need, so that all of us can be helped. Through Jesus Christ, our Lord we pray. Amen."**

"The Lord is good unto them that wait for Him, to the soul that seeketh Him."
Lamentations 3:25 (KJV)

In the silence that followed the prayer, both Emily and I sensed the presence of the Spirit of God. Both of us felt His peace. The anger and anxiety that pervaded the session prior to the prayer were gone. In an attitude of genuine concern for what a separation meant for Neal, Emily and I began to talk about how the separation could take place and yet take Neal's needs into consideration. We were no longer afraid that he would harm us. Emily

"We know not what we should pray for...but the Spirit itself maketh intercession for us."
Romans 8:26 (KJV)

and I trusted that God would honor our prayer and protect us. God did.

With the change in Emily's perception of how frightened Neal was about the separation, she successfully persuaded him that a change in their living arrangement would also benefit him. During the following months, Neal entered psychotherapy with another therapist, obtained a job, and moved out on his own. For the first time in years, he made friends with people his own age.

I shudder to think what might have happened had Emily and I tried to solve this problem on our own. God's response to our prayer went far beyond anything we could have envisioned in our moments of stress.

Confession and Repentance

All of us have sinned (1 John 1:8, 10). Sin separates us from God and interferes with our receiving His blessings. As I discussed in Chapter 4, sin is often a major source of our stress, especially the sins of pride and unforgiveness.

> *"If we confess our sins, He is faithful and just to forgive us our sins and to cleanse us from all unrighteousness"*
> 1 John 1:9 (KJV)

Repentance requires honesty and deep regret. When you and I ask for forgiveness, we must intend to refrain from sin. It should not be like we sometimes are with people when we say "excuse me" or "sorry" because that is expected and socially correct. No, our prayers of confession and repentance must be heartfelt.

Read the prayer of repentance found in Psalm 51:1-17. Meditate on what this Scripture specifically says to you. Pray your own prayer of repentance. If you can't remember any sin of commission or omission, ask the Holy Spirit to search your heart and bring to remembrance any unrepented sin in your life. Acknowledge your sin in prayer, repent and ask for God to forgive you. Then enjoy His peace.

"Search me, O God, and know my heart; try me, and know my thoughts: And lead me in the way everlasting."

Psalm 139:23-24 (KJV)

CRITERIA FOR EFFECTIVE PRAYERS

Whichever kind of prayer we pray, if we want them to work, i.e., to be effective, we need to meet several criteria.

1. We must love God and abide in Christ (John 15:7-11).

    This means that we must be steadfast in our love and commitment to Christ. If we only think of Him now and then, or primarily talk to Him when we are in trouble, our prayers and their results will be less successful. So, if we want to exper-ience the extraordinary benefits of

    "For the eyes of the Lord are on the righteous. And His ears are open to their prayers."

    1 Peter 3:12 (NKJ)

    prayer, *we must spend time communicating with God many times every day.*

2. We must be obedient to God's commandments.

    "And whatever we ask, we receive from Him, because we keep His commandments and do those things that are pleasing in His sight." **1 John 3:22 (KJV)**

3. If we love God, abide with Christ and obey God, we will of course ask Him for things that will be consistent with who He is and ask for things that He will be pleased to give to us. Even in our human

82

relationships, when we know a person well, we tend to know which of our requests she is more likely to grant and which not. The more we know God, the more on target we will be with our requests of Him.

"The effectual fervent prayer of a righteous man availeth much."
James 5:16 (KJV)

Sometimes, people's prayers are not answered because they *"pray amiss that they may spend it on their pleasure"* (James 4:3) For example:

Frederick fell in love with Mary. He prayed fervently that God would make her marry him. As time passed, he grew discouraged with God because he believed that God was not answering his prayer. Actually, God answered his prayer with a "No." Frederick prayed amiss because Mary was already married to someone else. God was not going to help Mary sin (Matthew 5:32). God was also not going to overpower Mary's will and "make" her fall in love with Frederick.

4. We must have faith that God will answer our prayers.

"Now faith is the substance of things hoped for, the evidence of things not seen." **Hebrews 11:1 (KJV)**

"Seek the Lord your God and you will find Him if you seek Him with all your heart and all your soul" **Deuteronomy 4:29 (KJV)**

In other words, faith means you trust and believe God and His promises, even if you can't verify His existence with your five senses.

When we trust God to answer our prayers, we can be at peace in the midst of great calamities. To me, this is the most precious medicine for reducing and managing stress.

Nevertheless, in spite of this, I must confess that my faith is stronger at some times than at others. Periodically, I find that I trust God more with some things than with others. But I praise God for His mercy. I've found that when my faith in Him is inadequate, I can ask Him to gift me with the amount of faith that I need. Since it pleases God for me to trust Him, I confidently ask Him for more faith. Each time He responds and increases my faith, I am then fortified to deal with my situation without getting stressed.

"The Lord is good to those whose hope is in Him, to the one who seeks Him."
Lamentations 3:25 (KJV)

"What things so ever ye desire, when ye pray, believe ye receive them and ye shall have them."
Mark 11:24 (KJV)

How to Make Praying a Habit

1. Before getting out of bed in the mornings, greet the Lord. In your own way say, "Good morning, Lord." Thank Him for something, i.e., for who He is, what He has done, what He is doing and what He will do, etc.

"His compassions fail not. They are new every morning, great is thy faithfulness."
Lamentations 3:22-23 (KJV)

2. Always say a prayer of thanksgiving at mealtimes. It is a privilege to have food and to be well enough to eat it.

3. Pray several times during the day and evening, even if your prayers are short.

4. When you see people in need or otherwise become aware of them, pray for them.

5. Each day pray for people in ministry, especially missionaries and others who may be in danger for

teaching and preaching the Gospel. Pray for our leaders in government.

6. Whatever your stressors, pray prayers of thanksgiving and petition. Thank God for making *all* things in your circumstances work for your good.

7. Pray for people who annoy you, offend you, or who are your enemies. Pray that God will bless them (Matthew 5:44). Pray also that He will enable you to love your enemies and to do good to them who hate you and despitefully use you (Matthew 5:44). When you do, God will bless you and give you a more positive attitude about them and your situation.

8. Whenever you begin to worry, interrupt that worry with a prayer of petition and thanksgiving. Pray specifically for what you want instead. Don't forget to thank God, in advance, for answering your prayer (Philipians 4:6-7).

9. Beam prayers of good will and blessings toward the people you meet today. I especially like to do this wherever I see children. When we beam a prayer, we are silently interceding for those who are unaware that we are praying for them. I have found that these prayers are like

"Let us therefore come boldly unto the throne of grace that we may obtain mercy, and find grace to help in time of need."
Hebrews 4:16 (KJV)

"Then shalt thou call, and the Lord shall answer; thou shalt cry, and He shalt say, Here I am."
Isaiah 58:9 (KJV)

"Pray to thy Father which is in secret and thy Father which seeth in secret shall reward thee openly."
Matthew 6:6 (KJV)

"Draw nigh to God, and He will draw nigh to you."
James 4:8 (KJV)

boomerangs. They seem to come back to also bless me.

10. Set aside regular times for extended prayers. Don't make it a habit to only speak to God on the run. Set aside time for leisurely praising, listening, and talking with God.

> *"Seek the Lord and His strength, seek His face continually."*
> 1 Chronicles 16:11 (KJV)

11. Always pray before going to sleep at night. Say prayers of praise, confession, repentance, thanksgiving, and intercession. These may be your last prayers on earth.

Prayer Makes a Difference

"The best medicine I've discovered is prayer," said a prominent physician to the British Medical Association. He went on to report that after spending his whole professional life treating sufferings of the mind, he said that "of all the hygienic measures to counteract disturbed sleep, depression of spirit, and a distressed mind, I would undoubtedly give first place to the simple habit of prayer than any other therapeutic agency known to man."

No matter how hectic your life may be, pray. You can pray anywhere and at any time. You can pray while you are getting dressed for work, while walking, while in the middle of a business meeting, or while holding a conversation.

> *"I am with thee, and will keep thee in all places whither thou goest."*
> Genesis 28:15 (KJV)

I agree with Thomas Kelly who believed we have the ability to order our mental life on more than one level at once. He asserted that on one level we may be thinking, discussing, seeing, calculating, and meeting all the demands of external affairs. Simultaneously, behind the scenes, at a profounder level, we may also be in prayer and adoration, song and worship in a gentle receptiveness to divine breathing.

Brother Lawrence, the monk who was known as the "the lord of all pots and pans" described how he prayed without ceasing. He commented that "the time of business does not with me differ from the time of prayer; and in the noise and clatter of my kitchen, while several persons are at the same time calling for different things, I possess God in as great tranquillity as if I were upon my knees at the blessed sacrament." Brother Lawrence urged us to "make a private chapel of our hearts where we can retire from time to time to commune with God peacefully, humbly, lovingly."

The unknown author of the following poem learned about the importance of taking time to pray.

The Difference

I got up early one morning
and rushed right into the day.
I had so much to accomplish
that I didn't have time to pray.

Problems just tumbled about me
and heavier came each task.
"Why doesn't God help me? I wondered.
He said, "But you didn't ask."

I wanted to see joy and beauty,
but the day toiled on, gray and bleak.
I wondered why God didn't show me.
He said "But you didn't seek."

I tried to come into God's presence.
I used all my keys at the lock.
God gently and lovingly chided,
"My child, you didn't knock."

I woke up early this morning
and paused before entering the day
I had so much to accomplish
that I had to take time to pray.

Pray and allow God to show His great love for you. Talk to Him about your stressors. Let Him help you to triumph over them.

"Continue earnestly in prayer, being vigilant in it with thanksgiving."
Colossians 4:2 (NKJ)

REMEMBER

1. Prayer is an essential part of a fervent love relationship with God.

2. Regularly pray a variety of prayers. Among them should be prayers of:

    ❖ Praise and Adoration

    ❖ Thanksgiving

    ❖ Petition and Supplication

    ❖ Intercession

    ❖ Confession and Repentance

3. Pray about the little and big things of life.
4. Be sure to seek and listen to the guidance of the Holy Spirit.
5. Make praying a reflexive response to life.

Principle 6

BE STILL

"Be still and know that I am God"

Psalms 46:10 (KJV)

It is so easy to keep on the go. Our jobs, families, friends, special interests and social activities can make life stressful, even if we are having fun with all that we do.

God knew that if He left it to most of us, we would work, play hard or otherwise keep busy almost all of the time. He knew that if He didn't tell some of us to chill out, cool down, be still that we would be like the bunny that runs on the Ever Ready battery and eventually burn ourselves out in the process.

Sabbath

God prescribed a weekly rest for His people. He said,

"Six days shall thou labor and do all thy work. The seventh is the Sabbath. In it thou shall not do any labor."

Exodus 20:8-11

This mandatory rest day is sacred to Him. It seems that many Christians do not take the Sabbath seriously. We may go to church and spend the day enjoying family and friends.

But most of us do not make Sunday a deliberate day of rest and renewal.

After deciding to take the idea of a weekly day of rest seriously, I found that I could manage stress much more effectively than when I worked seven days a week. When I say work, I don't mean showing up at a job. My work could include thinking, studying, cleaning the house, shopping and the like. I decided that I wanted to explore the potential benefits to me of working only six days and resting on the seventh. Jesus taught that the Sabbath was made for mankind. I therefore decided that I wanted to personally experience some of these benefits.

My Christian affiliation did not require that I adhere to restrictions practiced by people of other Christian traditions. I decided that my Sabbath meant that I would go to church, not cook, do housework or any professional work. I choose Sundays because that is the day that I normally go to church. Usually, I enjoy a meal with my family at a restaurant. I take a long nap, have a leisurely conversation with God and, later in the evenings, I read or watch television. At other times, I drive to the beach and while delighting in the sight and smell of the Pacific Ocean, I talk and listen to God.

I find that on Mondays, I am more rested, refreshed and creative than I could ever have been had I continued working all weekend. In fact, the quality of my work is better after taking the Sabbath. I recommend that you do the same.

It won't always be easy to observe a Sabbath. Not only will you have to use your will power to refrain from doing whatever "work" you had the habit of doing, you may also find that the people in your life will need to be trained to take your Sabbath day seriously. I have been lucky that my husband and children have been very respectful of my rest on Sundays, whether I'm at home or at the ocean.

Sleep

Experts tell us that most Americans suffer from some sort of sleep deprivation. It seems that many of us get less than the recommended seven to nine hours of sleep per night. When we deprive ourselves of regular and restful sleep, we find it more difficult to concentrate, we make more mistakes, are more easily irritated and fatigued.

I have had to learn to listen to my body. It definitely protests when I deprive it of the restful sleep it needs. Through experimentation, I've found that my mind, body and emotions work best if I have eight to nine hours of sleep per night. I highly recommend that you let your mind, emotions and body tell you at what level of sleep they optimally function. The goal is optimal functioning, not what you can get away with. I've met people who boast that they only need five hours of sleep. Many of them are quite "uptight", impatient people. In short, they appear to me to be people

"It is vain to rise up early. To sit up late, To eat the bread of sorrows: For so He gives His beloved sleep"

Psalm 127:2 (NKJV)

who have lived with chronic stress so long, that it feels quite normal to them. I know that we humans have different needs, but I think that we manage stress better when we give our bodies the sleep they need

Naps and Other Rest Periods

I am grateful that I can become rested and refreshed with naps. I feel compassion for people who either can't take naps or actually feel more tired after taking them. I recommend that, if you can fit a nap into your daily schedule that you do so.

If you can't, for whatever reason, take short periods of rest during your day, you may have to experiment with what feels restful to you. Some people sit quietly for fifteen or more minutes in the morning and later during the day.

Jesus and His apostles took time to rest. Mark 6:30-31 tells us: *"The apostles now returned to Jesus from their tour and told Him all they had done and what they had said to the people they visited. Then Jesus suggested, 'Let's get away from the crowd for a while and rest."* Undoubtedly, these periods of rest were important to Jesus and the disciples in managing the stress inherent in their vocation.

I have found that these brief periods of daily rest are so important to my stress management, that to insure that I take them during my otherwise, very busy day, I actually schedule times for them on my calendar. If I don't protect those times, I can easily fill them with telephone calls, seeing clients, reading, writing or doing some other chores that increase my stress.

Vacations

Some people regard vacations as pure luxuries. In a sense, they are. Not everyone can afford to be away from work for extended periods of time. But vacations can be enormously helpful in managing stress.

During a vacation, you have the opportunity to be in a different environment. Just the change of scenery can take your mind off of daily worries and responsibilities. If you are able to spend time in a different environment with people you enjoy, by all means do so. Not only can your spirits be lifted, but you may actually develop new perspectives on your life, that better equip you to deal with any challenges you encounter.

Keep in mind that even if you can't afford to leave town for a vacation, you might spend time in a park that you haven't visited before, spend time with a friend, or pretend that you are a tourist visiting your city for the first time. Look at its architecture, visits its museums and other attractions or just sit and watch people passing by.

If you can afford to travel out of town, do it. Make sure to connect with friendly people and with nature's beauty. Frequent times of rest, relaxation and renewal can greatly enhance your ability to live a more stress-resistant life-style.

Quiet Your Body

The Scriptures tell us that we are *"fearfully and wonderfully made."* (Psalm 139:13-14) One of the many times that this assertion hits home is when we experience the stress relieving benefits of quieting our bodies.

To quiet your body, assess where your muscles are tense. Are you grinding your teeth? Is your breathing shallow? If you find tension in any part of your body, simply tell your muscles to relax. You can give a general order to your body to "relax" or you can focus on each separate group of muscles and silently say "relax". For example, you could focus your thoughts on your upper left arm. After telling it to relax, you could then concentrate on your lower left arm, and then tell it to relax before doing the same with your upper right arm, etc. Slowly focus on other parts of your body and think "relax." At the end of this process your body should be significantly less tensed.

If at first, you don't experience a great deal of relaxation, don't get discourage. With practice you should improve.

A faster way to train your body to relax, is to simultaneously tense all of your muscles. Ball your fists, frown, push your chest out as far as it will go, while tightening your abdomen, stretching your legs and pointing your toes.. Hold this position for several minutes. Then slowly let go and relax. Pay attention to how your muscles feel when they are tense and when they are relaxed. With practice, your muscles will remember what "relax" feels like and will promptly obey your silent commands.

Quiet Your Mind

Learning to quiet our thoughts is an important way to reduce stress and increase our peace of mind. This is especially important when we need to stop our minds from racing from one stress inducing thought to another.

Prayer is an extremely effective means of quieting the mind. I find that filling my mind with praise for God, and thanksgiving for the many blessings He bestows upon me helps to calm my mind and emotions.

"Truly my soul silently waits for God;..."

Psalms 62:1 (NKJV)

I have found that it is helpful to just sit or lie quietly with an attitude of quiet expectation. In those moments, I wait for God to speak to my spirit. I don't censure my thoughts, I let them come. If they are anxious thoughts, I follow the recommendation of Philippians 4:6-8 that declares

"Be anxious for nothings, but with prayer, supplication and thanksgiving, make your request known unto God.

*And the peace of God which passes all understanding will
guard your heart and your mind through Christ Jesus."*

I regard this scripture as God's prescription for
stopping anxious thoughts. This form of thought stopping
requires us to deliberately interrupt our stressful thoughts
and focus instead on what we want rather than what we fear.
When, in faith, we thank God, in advance, for responding to
our prayers, we can experience His unique peace that passes
all understanding.

Sometimes, I don't know what I want instead of what I
fear. At those times I ask the Holy Spirit to pray on my behalf.
Romans 8:26-28 teaches that:

*"...the Spirit also helps in our weaknesses. For we do not
know what we should pray for as we ought, but the Spirit
Himself makes intercession for us with groanings which
cannot be uttered. Now He who searches the hearts knows
what the mind of the Spirit is, because He makes
intercession for the saints according to the will of God. And
we know that all things work together for good to those who
love God to those who are the called according to His
purpose."*

Even when my mind is not filled with anxious thoughts,
I have found it helpful to quiet it by concentrating on my
breathing. I never cease to be amazed at how wonderfully
made we are!. God made us so that we can grow calmer
through the simple act of slow deep breathing. You and I can
do this anywhere. Just slowly inhale through your nose and
fill your lungs. Hold your breath for the mental count of five.
Then for a count of five, slowly exhale. Slowly repeat this five
or more times. Pay attention to filling up, holding and letting
go. Reverend Jeremiah Wright, of Chicago, Illinois, does an

effective variation of this deep breathing. As he exhales, he thinks, "Lord, I need you." While he slowly inhales, he thinks, "Lord, I receive you." He repeats this until he feels his tensions melt away.

You too you may find that slow deep breathing not only quiets your mind, but also your spirit and prepares you for a deeper experience of God.

Knowing God in the Stillness

The primary purpose of becoming still is for us to know God more intimately. It is relatively easy to assert intellectually that God is with us. We get this information from reading the Bible and listening to sermons. We can experience Him with us at any time, because He *is* always with us. However, when we stop being distracted by our busy lives and deliberately make time for a rendezvous with Him, God reveals Himself to us more fully.

It is in the stillness that our spirits can better hear the "still small voice of God." What this means to me is that through the Holy Spirit, God speaks to us, revealing His ability to meet all of our needs. (Philippians 4:19). Although God loves you and me, the way He communicates this truth to each of us is customized to fit our level of faith, love, understanding, spiritual maturity and circumstances. These encounters with God can transform us. One of the benefits of this transformation is the deepening of our faith and the strengthening of our abilities to manage whatever stresses come our way.

In these encounters, God often reveals His will for us. In their book, *Experiencing God,* Henry T. Blackaby and Claude V. King wrote, "The testimony of the Bible from Genesis to

Revelation is that God speaks to His people. In our day, God speaks to us through the Holy Spirit. He uses the Bible, prayer, circumstances and the church (other believers). No one of these methods of God's speaking is, by itself, a clear indicator of God's directions. But when God says the same thing through each of these ways, you can have confidence to proceed."[1]

I have found that sometimes God's instructions to me, initially, increased my stress. There were times when He invited me to do something that required me to trust Him more deeply than I had until then. For example, in one of our silent rendezvous, I sensed that God wanted me to give up my teaching position at a major university. That frightened me. It meant that I had to relinquish tenure, which in my mind meant "job security." The fact that God was calling me, was not remarkable. I was aware of Biblical accounts of God calling believers like Abraham, Moses, Noah, Jonah and Paul. I wish that I could tell you that I promptly obeyed God. But I didn't. It took me more than two years. During that period, God repeated His instructions.

Part of my hesitation to obey was that I was not entirely sure that I was hearing Him. I asked several believers to pray for me to hear God clearly. Three of those who agreed to pray, later told me that they were sure that God wanted me to leave the university and that He had a special work for me to do which required that I leave. None of these people knew the others. So when the third person told me in almost the same

1   Blackaby, Henry & King, Claude, *Experiencing God*, Nashville, Tennessee, Broadman & Holman Publishers, 1994 p. 56

words as the other two, I became convinced that leaving the university was God's will for me. I finally obeyed. As a result, my life is more meaningful and joyous.

My subsequent experiences were consistent with Blackaby's & King's assertion that "God is going to be revealing Himself so you can trust Him and have faith in Him. He is going to reveal His purposes so you will be involved in His work rather than some other work. He reveals His ways so you can accomplish His purpose in a way that will glorify Him. God's ways are not our ways. You cannot discover these truths about God on your own. Truth is revealed."[2]

Ask yourself what implications does God's commandment that His people observe a weekly Sabbath have for how you are managing your life?

How often do you take time to rest and to get the sleep you need?

Do you regularly take time to be still, relax your body, quiet your mind and rendezvous with God to know Him more intimately and to receive the message He has for you?

2   Ibid. 56

REMEMBER

1. Take weekly Sabbaths during which you rest and worship God.

2. Get the amount of sleep your body requires, every night.

3. Take short rest periods daily.

4. Learn to reduce bodily tensions.

5. Regularly meditate or otherwise, quiet your mind.

6. Regularly enjoy the knowledge that comes from intimacy with God in silent times.

Now let's see how by developing a godly self-love, you can better manage stress.

Principle 7

LOVE YOURSELF

"You shall love…yourself"
Mark 12:13 (NKJV)

I often wonder why Jesus set self-love as the standard for loving others. He said that the second greatest commandment is "Love your neighbor *as* you love yourself." Jesus certainly knows about people whose love of themselves is damaged. He knows that the lack of healthy self-love causes people to:

❖ have low self-esteems and relate to others in ways that damage their own and others' self- respect;

❖ be proned to depressions and be unresponsive to other people or withdraw from them altogether;

❖ frequently make decisions that are harmful to themselves and to others;

❖ gravitate toward or actively seek dangerous situations and abusive relationships which can be destructive and sometimes fatal;

❖ be prone to have physical and/or mental illnesses, which spoil the quality of their lives and those of family and friends;

❖ be unable to love other people in ways that are healthy and thereby inflict emotional scars that get passed on from generation to generation.

The quality of our love for others is marred when we have serious deficits in our love for ourselves.

There are a variety of reasons why some people do not love themselves.

❖ Some had parents or other caretakers who did not love them; therefore, they were not taught how to love themselves.

❖ Some had parents who hated them and taught them self- hatred.

❖ Others had parents or caretakers who used harsh discipline or abused them physically, sexually, or emotionally. Consequently, these people believe that they are bad, dirty, and unworthy of love, even their own.

"Parents do not provoke your children to wrath, but bring them up in the training and admonition of the Lord".

Ephesians 6:4 (NKJV)

❖ Some come from "religious" traditions that teach self-love is equivalent to pride, vanity, egotistical selfishness, and is, therefore, a sin. They equate self-loathing with holiness.

❖ Some people made colossal mistakes or committed what they think are unforgivable sins. All of which leaves them feeling guilty, ashamed, and unworthy of their own or anyone else's love.

"Out of the same mouth proceed blessing and cursing. My brethren these things ought not to be so."

James 3:10 (NKJV)

Whatever the reasons some of us may have for not loving ourselves, the consequences for our relationships with God, others, and ourselves are serious. Love deficits makes us more vulnerable to stress. God wants to heal us. *God wants us to love whom and what He loves. God loves you and me. Therefore, we should also love ourselves and each other.*

"Therefore be imitators of God as dear children. And walk in love, as Christ also has loved us and given Himself for us...."
Ephesians5: 1-2 (NKJV)

What Is Godly Self-Love?

The Bible tells us:

> *Love is patient, love is kind. It does not envy, it does not boast, it is not proud. It is not rude, it is not self-seeking, it is not easily angered, it keeps no record of wrongs. Love does not delight in evil but rejoices with the truth. It always protects, always trust, always hopes, always perseveres. Love never fails.* **1 Corinthians 13:4-8**

Notice that never once does this scripture say that the existence of love depends upon the characteristics or behaviors of the person who is loved. This love, which is called *agape*, is unconditional

Let us look at how *agape* love of ourselves helps us to either avoid, diminish, or better manage various stresses.

"Therefore, if anyone is in Christ, he is a new creation; old things have passed away; behold all things have become new."
2 Corinthians 5:17 (NKJV)

Be Patient with Yourself

All of us need to learn to be patient with ourselves. You and I can become anxious, angry, and distressed about our imperfections. I do not mean to suggest that you should deny your shortcomings or merely shrug off your faults with a "Well, that's just the way I am." On the contrary, you and I should acknowledge our faults without berating ourselves and seek God's help to eradicate them.

"The Lord is good to those who wait for Him, To the soul who seeks Him."
Lamentations 3:25

Otherwise, our impatience with ourselves makes us prone to perfectionism. Demanding perfection of ourselves, places impossible and, sometimes, unbearable burdens on us. For example, Lena said that after making mistakes, she feels so badly that she tells herself, "If I can't be perfect, I will not *be* at all." Lena attempted suicide five times.

"And therefore will the Lord wait, that he may be gracious unto you, and therefore will He be exalted, that he may have mercy upon you; for the Lord is a God of judgement; blessed are all they that wait for him."
Isaiah 30:18 (NKJV)

We will live more stress-resistant lives when we adopt the attitude that God has towards us. He has high standards for us, but He is patient with us (Romans 5:15). To develop patience with ourselves and with our stressful situations we should:

1. Trust God

Pray and ask for an outcome that will please Him. If you can reduce the stress in ways that are consistent with the Word of God, do so. If a distressing situation takes time or is truly beyond your control, wait patiently for God to change the situation

"Commit your way to the Lord; Trust also in Him, And He shall bring it to pass."
Psalm 37:5 (KJV)

and/or to change you. Don't become stressed by the "Divine delay."

For example, years ago I was upset that God did not grant me a child. It was not until fourteen years later that I became a mother! But I now praise God that He did not give me what I wanted at that time. His plan was infinitely better. During that fourteen-year "wait" many

"My soul wait silently for God above, For my expectation is from Him."

Psalm 62:5 (KJV)

circumstances of my life improved. I matured so that I was able to become a better mother than I ever could have been at that earlier time.

Repeatedly, Scripture exhorts us to "wait upon the Lord" (Psalm 62:5; Proverbs 20:22; Hosea 12:6). We can develop this ability to wait by deciding to trust God and not to fret. If your faith falters, ask God to help you to trust Him.

2. Develop a Joyful Attitude

The Bible actually tells us to be happy about our stressors! The Scriptures ask:

> "...is your life full of difficulties and temptations? Then be happy for when the way is rough, your patience has a chance to grow. So let it grow, and don't try to squirm out of your problems. For when your patience is finally in full bloom, then you will be ready for anything, strong in character, full and complete."

> **James 1:2-4 (LBV)**

"But let all those rejoice who put their trust in You; Let them ever shout for joy, because You defend them; Let those also who love Your name Be joyful in You. For You, O Lord, will bless the righteous; With favor You will surround him as with a shield."

Psalm 5:11-12 (NKJV)

105

I find that my patience increases as I remember that each frustration, problem, or painful experience offers me the opportunity to trust God and to rely upon Him for guidance and comfort. My stress is minimized and sometime eradicated whenever I remember:

"Always give thanks for everything to our God and father in the name of our Lord Jesus Christ."
Ephesians 5:20 (NIV)

"...We know that all that happens to us is working for our good if we love God and are fitting into His plans."
Romans 8:28 (NIV)

I read this Scripture to Katherine, a mother whose son committed suicide several years ago and whose daughter developed an incurable brain disease the following year. I asked Katherine if she perceived any good that grew from these catastrophes.

"I thank You and praise You, O God. You have given me wisdom and might..."
Daniel 2:23 (NKJV)

She thought for a moment. "Yes," she said, " I used to be a mean mother. I think the way I treated my son when he was a child ultimately contributed to his suicide. After he died, I decided to be a nicer person, and I am. I don't get so angry and say nasty things to people like I used to.... I like myself better these days." Katherine went on to say, "The good that's come from my daughter's illness is that I'm closer to her son, my five-year old grandson whom I'm helping to raise. I give him the patience and guidance I did not give my own children when they were young. I have a

"Now we exhort you...warn those who are unruly, Comfort the fainthearted, uphold the weak, be patient with all. See that no one renders evil for evil to anyone, but always pursue what is good for your selves and for all."
Thessalonians 5:14,15 (NKJV)

good relationship with him," she said, smiling.

She continued, "Another good that is growing out of my daughter's illness is that, although it is very painful to see her, I visit her at the convalescent home two or three times a week. I talk and play games with her. I make sure that the staff treats her well. I pray a lot," she calmly said. "God helps me to endure all of this."

Be Kind to Yourself

It is possible to get so caught up in being helpful and kind to others that we neglect to be kind to ourselves. Eventually we feel misused or exploited. When you love yourself in a healthy way, you actively do good things to and for yourself. God shows His love for you through kindness. Likewise, be kind to yourself.

"Tell those who are rich not to be proud and not to trust in their money, which will soon be gone, but their pride and trust should be in the living God, who always richly gives us all we need for our enjoyment."
1 Timothy 6:17 (LB)

My mother-in-law, Ruby Love, is a kind woman who goes out of her way to do good things for other people. For eight years she effectively managed the stresses of caring for her invalid husband. Recently, many friends and relatives died. Yet she is even- tempered, friendly, and peaceful. I asked her what she does when she wants to be kind to herself. She answered that she:

"This is the day the Lord has made. Let us rejoice and be glad in it."
Psalm 118:24 (LB)

- ❖ Goes out to lunch with friends.
- ❖ Reads a book.
- ❖ Travels
- ❖ Sleeps late
- ❖ Buys a pretty blouse

❖ Sees a movie

She ended by saying, "I am kind to myself when I do something kind for other people. I feel good when I am kind."

Like my mother-in-law, you and I like and love ourselves better when we are kind people. Our graciousness, compassion, and generosity enhance our self-esteems. Our kindness reflects the Spirit of God who enables us to deal confidently with whatever stressors we encounter.

Take time now to:

❖ Prayerfully examine the degree to which you are a kind to yourself and to others.

❖ Ask God to reveal to you how by being more kind to other people and to yourself, you will minimize, eradicate, or better manage your stress.

❖ Decide specific kind things you will do for others and do them.

❖ Decide specific kind things you will do for yourself and do them.

"...do good,...be rich in good deeds and...be generous and willing to share. In this way...lay up treasures...as a firm foundation for the coming age, so that (you) may take hold of the life that is truly life."

1 Timothy 6:18,19 (LB)

"He has made everything beautiful in its time. He has also set eternity in the hearts of men...I know that there is nothing better for men than to be happy and do good while they live. That everyone may eat and drink and find satisfaction in all his toil - this is the gift of God."

Ecclesiastes 3:11-12 (NIV)

Do Not Be Envious

Life has obvious inequities. People vary in their talents, strengths, educations, family circumstances, beauty, money, opportunities, and the like. If you or I respond to these inequities with envy, we entertain unholy passions, which will definitely rob us of God's peace. When we are jealous and begrudge others for what they have, we stress ourselves with resentment, anger, and discontent.

When we ask God to help us to truly love ourselves, we cooperate with the process to replace our envy, resentment, and fiercely competitive attitudes with contentment and appreciation for what He has already given us. We will actively look for and develop our own God-given uniqueness, talents, and interests.

Take a moment now and record in your journal some of the ways you are "fearfully and wonderfully made" (Psalm 139:14). List some of the abilities, talents (however modest they seem to you), and opportunities that God has given you. Ask family and friends to help you to identify these unique blessings. Prayerfully consider how you

"...for I have learned to be content whatever, the circumstances. I know what it is to be in need, and I know what it is to have plenty. I have learned the secret of being content in any and every situation, whether well fed or hungry, whether living in plenty or in want. I can do everything through him who gives me strength."

Philippians 4:11-13 (NIV)

"Because your lovingkindness is better than life, my lips shall praise You. Thus I will bless You while I live."

Psalm 63:3 (NKJV)

"O Lord, how manifold are Your works! In wisdom You have made them all."

Psalm 104:24 (NKJV)

may use them. The more you develop and use your gifts and talents, the more you will enjoy life.

> For example: "Sylvester has a high pressure job. He battles depression and has difficulty loving himself. In a therapy session, he revealed that as a teenager, he loved to paint with watercolors. He said, that he used to be very good at it. I encouraged him to paint in the evenings, instead of taking work home. He did. Several weeks later, he showed me a few of his paintings. They were beautiful. "I'm so glad I started painting again," he said. "I thank God I can still paint. Since I've been painting, I'm more relaxed."

Do Not Be Boastful

When we "toot our own horns" other people may become envious and resent us. If we have a godly self-love, we avoid stressing ourselves by needlessly eliciting other people's hostilities.

Do Not Be Proud

As we previously discussed, pride is a sin that alienates us from God and other people. We need His help and often the help of other people to effectively manage, or in some instances, to avoid stress altogether. With healthy self-love we won't let pride deprive us of the love, comfort,

"Better is the sight of the eyes than the wanderings of desire. This also is vanity and grasping for the wind."
Ecclesiastes 6:9 (NKJV)

"Lord, all my desire is before you; And my sighing is not hidden from You."
Psalm 38:9 (NKJV)

"I will boast of all his kindness to me. Let all who are discouraged take heart. Let us praise the Lord together, and exalt his name."
Psalm 34:2 (LB)

"Arise, O Lord; O God, lift up thine hand; forget not the humble."
Psalm 10:12

and help that our humble attitudes will motivate others to give us.

There is an important difference between humility and low self-esteem. Humble people do not aggressively seek other people's attention and adulation. When, however, other people compliment them, humble people accept the goodwill graciously and without fanfare. On the other hand, the person with low self-esteem becomes extremely uncomfortable and protests the compliment. For example, that person asks "You like this old sweater?" then goes on to imply that something is wrong with you for admiring the sweater!

"The humble shall see their God at work for them. No wonder they will be so glad! All who seek for God shall live in joy."
Psalm 69:32 (LB)

"Blessed are the meek, for they shall inherit the earth."
Matthew 5:5 (KIV)

Do Not Be Rude

As people who have passionate love relationships with God, we try to never be rude to someone God loves. That would indirectly be rude and offensive to God (Matthew 25:40). Since God loves us all, you and I must not be rude to anyone, including ourselves.

"Let your speech always be with grace..."
Colossians 4:6 (NKJV)

We contribute to our stress when we treat or speak of ourselves disrespectfully. For example, if you call yourself "stupid" or some other derogatory name, you show a lack of respect for yourself. Your rudeness will inevitably make you feel more upset, depressed and discouraged, all of which are stress inducing emotions.

"Keep your tongue from evil, And your lips from speaking deceit."
Psalm 34:13 (NKJV)

Also, when you are rude to yourself, you, by example, teach others to treat you the same way. Always speak respectfully to and of yourself. You will develop more self-respect, an invaluable resource for dealing with stress.

Do Not Be Self Seeking

People will resent us, if we are self-centered power freaks, who are manipulative or domineering. Sooner or later our relationships with other people will suffer. Some may cease to love us or abandon us altogether. Then we will experience the distress of loneliness.

"Do nothing from selfishness or empty conceit but with humility of mind let each of you regard one another as more important than himself; do not merely look out for your own interests but also for the interests of others."
Philippians 2:3,4 (NIV)

Do Not Be Easily Provoked

Each of us needs to learn what are our "hot buttons," i.e. those things about which we become irritated, touchy, or hostile. Take a moment now and make a list of the things that irk you, are pet peeves, or "bug" you.

For each of the things, about which you tend to become provoked, ask yourself:

"A hot-tempered man stirs up strife, But the slow to anger pacifies contention."
Proverbs 15:18 (NIV)

❖ How important is this issue to God? Why?

❖ Am I only looking at things from my own perspective?

❖ What do I need to find out in order to see this issue from the other person's perspective?

"...let everyone be quick to hear, slow to speak and slow to anger."
James 1:19 (RSV)

112

❖ What are other, more productive, and loving ways that I can respond to this issue? (Name at least three.)

Prayerfully consider how to diffuse your "hot buttons" and bring them under your control (Galatians 5:22-23). As you develop better self-discipline, you will grow in godly self-love and confidence. These are powerful resources for combating stress related to anger.

Do Not Hold Grudges

Unforgiveness is an acid that eats away one's peace of mind. Keeping a record of the wrongs others have done condemns you to mentally reliving the offenses. As you repeatedly review past hurts, you renew your anger and sense of victimization. Consequently your stress level increases. We become more stress resistant when we quickly forgive others and refuse to hold grudges.

It is also crucial that we forgive ourselves. When we sincerely ask God to forgive us for our wrong doings, we are guaranteed that He will (1 John 1:9). Then we must imitate God and forgive ourselves. This frees the energy that would, otherwise, be bound up by guilt, self-reproach, and regrets. With our released energy, we will have more stamina, drive, and confidence to better deal with stress and anything else encountered in our lives.

"For thou, Lord art good and ready to forgive, And abundant in loving-kindness to all who call upon thee."

Psalms 86:5 (KJV)

Do Not Delight in Evil

At one time or another, we have all met a Pitiful Paul, Crying Clara, Sad Saul, or Vicki, the Victim. These people enjoy

113

regaling us with stories about how much they've suffered, what terrible mistakes they've made, or how nothing ever works out for them. They tend to be people who are chronically stressed.

As we learn to develop godly self-love, we refuse to be like them and wallow in self-pity, entertaining others with accounts of our inadequacies and problems. This does not mean that we don't selectively share our problems and concerns with others who love God. We may need other people's wise counsel or practical help to reduce or manage our stress.

> *"...wisdom preserves the lives of its possessors ."*
> **Ecclesiastes 7:12b (NIV)**

Rejoice in the Truth

When you love God and yourself, you will always try to be truthful and sincere. Lying can cause us stress.

When you and I rejoice in the truth, we will be willing to learn the truth about ourselves. The more that you are willing to greet whatever you learn about yourself with loving compassion, the more easily you will get to know yourself. When we are harsh, perfectionistic, or unforgiving of ourselves, it is as though parts of our personalities hide from us. When our search for self-knowledge (truth) is undertaken in a spirit of kindness and respect, we are able to gain important insights into who we really are. Many times self-knowledge greatly aids us in dealing with stress. For example:

> *"Do not lie to one another...."*
> **Colossians 3:9 (NKJV)**

When 32-year-old Ingrid found out that she was pregnant with Oskar's child, she was devastated. During the ten months of their affair, she felt guilty about their sexual relations. They had mutually decided that they were incompatible and had ended their relationship two weeks before Ingrid learned of the pregnancy.

Oskar felt certain that if they married because of the pregnancy, they would be very unhappy.

"...Now this body is not for fornication, but for the lord; and the Lord for the body."

1 Corinthians 6:13 (KJV)

In her therapy sessions, Ingrid sorted out her guilt, shame, and disappointment with Oskar. Ingrid decided to give birth and raise the child as a single parent. She, nevertheless, was greatly troubled that she had been "stupid enough to get pregnant."

"Is this your first pregnancy?" I asked.

"Yes," Ingrid answered. "Although I've been sexually active since college, I've never gotten pregnant. In fact, " she continued, "I often wondered if I could ever get pregnant."

"That's interesting," I said, "why do you think that after so many years of keeping yourself from getting pregnant, you got pregnant now."

Startled by my question, Ingrid thought awhile. "It was an accident," she offered.

I smiled.

"You think it wasn't?" she asked.

"What do you think?" I responded.

She became silent and introspective.

"You are truly my disciples if you live as I tell you to and you will know the truth, and the truth will set you free."

John 8:31-32 (LB)

"I guess there was a part of me that wanted a baby," she admitted. "I had been feeling that it was time for me to settle down and have someone to live for other than just myself."

Once Ingrid faced the truth about herself, she began to feel better. Over the next months, she grew happier and *more relaxed as she planned for her baby. As a Christian, she acknowledged and repented of her sin of fornication. She accepted God's forgiveness, forgave herself, and significantly reduced her stress.*

Our willingness to face the truth about ourselves is essential to being authentic people. Personal integrity goes a long way in helping us to love and respect ourselves.

Always Protect

Our godly self-love means that you and I protect ourselves physically, mentally, and emotionally. We show appreciation to God by being good stewards of the minds, emotions and bodies He has given us.

Always Trust and Hope

Loving ourselves with a godly self-love means that we give ourselves the benefit of the doubt. We develop positive and optimistic attitudes towards ourselves. We can more readily do this when our relationship with God is very strong. What we really trust is His work in us as He transforms us into the image of His beloved Son, Jesus Christ. When we are trusting and we affirm His work in us, we love the persons we are becoming. This sense of well being helps us immeasurably as we encounter the stressors of our lives.

Always Persevere

When you and I have godly self-love, we won't give up on ourselves. In the course of our lives, we will inevitably encounter obstacles to being the kind of people God wants us to be. We need to remember, Paul's admonition in Galatians 6:9:

"And let us not grow weary while doing good, for in due season we shall reap if we do not lose heart." **(NIV)**

To really love ourselves, we develop the same attitude that God has towards us. HE NEVER GIVES UP ON US! His love for us never fails. And we should not fail to love ourselves in a godly manner.

REMEMBER

1. Develop a godly self-love. It is the foundation of your mental health.

2. Be patient with yourself.

3. Be kind to yourself.

4. Don't allow envy, rudeness, boastfulness, self-centeredness or evil to be components of your character.

5. Be a truthful and positive person.

6. Never give up on yourself. God doesn't

Principle 8

LOVE OTHERS

"Love thy neighbor...."
Mark 12:31 (KJV)

Even in a world where there were no traffic jams, urban crimes, terrorism, AIDS, declining economies, or racial tensions, the first man, Adam, needed a support system.

> *"And the Lord said, 'It isn't good for man to be alone, I will make a companion for him, a helper, suited to his needs."*
> **Genesis 2:18 (LB)**

God gave Adam another human, Eve, to live with him in loving intimacy. Modern science has discovered that, like Adam, it is not good for any of us to be alone, without human love connections. Researchers have scientific evidence that people who have friends and close family relationships are generally happier and have less stress than those who do not. Other people can help us prevent, reduce, or better manage stress by giving us love, comfort, advice, information, money and other tangible resources. These people often lend helping hands with chores, nurse us

"Two can accomplish more than twice as much as one, for the results can be much better. If one falls, the other pulls him up; but if a man falls when he is alone, he's in trouble."
Ecclesiastes 4:9-10 (LB)

118

when we are sick and connect us with resources we need.

We are more likely to have these helpful relationships when we have loving attitudes toward people. When we have passionate love relationships with God and love ourselves in a godly manner, we are better equipped to truly love other people. As we discussed in the previous chapter, 1 Corinthians 13:4-7 describes the standards of the kind of love that we are to have for others and for ourselves. In Principle 7, we discussed the specific characteristics of godly self-love. We are commanded to love other people like that, as well. Christ does not command that we feel a rush of passionate joy each time we encounter others. Rather, He tells us to maintain a benevolent, *Agape* attitude towards people. This loving mind-set is crucial to our having right relationships with God, others and ourselves.

"Dear friends, let us love one another, for love comes from God. Everyone who loves has been born of God and knows God. Whoever does not love does not know God, because God is love... since God so loved us, we also ought to love one another. No one has ever seen God; but if we love each other, God lives in us and His love is made complete in us."

"Be kindly affectionate one to another with brotherly love; in honor preferring one another."

Romans 12:10 (KJ)

1 John 4:7-8; 11-12 (NIV)

You probably already know how much better you feel when you have loving relationships with family, friends, co-workers, and neighbors. But as daughters and sons of God, we also need to love people other than our families and friends.

Be Kind

God, who is kind to us, is pleased when He finds that quality in us. Kindness is a sign that His Holy Spirit abides in us (Galatians 5:22).

To really love God, other people, and ourselves, we must constantly try to be kind. When we are kind, we cooperate with the Holy Spirit in transforming us into friendly compassionate people. We ask for God's help to be like Him and to be kind even to our enemies and to those who hate and curse us (Matthew 5:44). We look to God, our Father, not other people to reward our kindness. Some people may reject and dislike us for our kindness, but most people will return our kindness with love and gratitude. As a kind person you will find that other people are more willing to help you with whatever stressors you may encounter.

> *"And whatever you do, do it heartily, as to the Lord and not to men."*
> Colossians 3:23 (NKJV)

> *"Since you have been chosen by God who has given you this new kind of life, and because of this deep love and concern for you, you should practice tenderhearted mercy and kindness to others."*
> Colossians 3:12 (LB)

One of the ways that we can be kind is by showing compassion and generosity to people who are less fortunate than ourselves (Matthew 6:1-4). No matter what you are going through, or how difficult your stressful situation seems, there are people somewhere who have more difficulties than you. One of the paradoxes of life is that if you help someone else, you are often helped in the process. When you and I help other people, our minds are taken off our own situations. That distraction can bring us much needed rest from our own problems. In some cases, as we help others, we gain new knowledge and develop new perspectives, which help us with our own stress. There is also another benefit to us. Jesus said:

> "Give and it shall be given to you. A good measure, pressed down, shaken together and running over, will be poured into your lap. For with the measure you use, it will be measured to you." **Luke 6:38 (NIV)**

I understand this Scripture to mean that when we generously give anything—our time, money, comfort, love, and the like, that it will be returned to us in abundance. We may not always receive from the same people that we give to, but we will receive from someone. I also understand this Scripture to mean that when we give criticism, unkindness, bitterness, and the like, these things will also be returned to us in abundance! The Apostle Paul warns:

> "Do not be deceived: God cannot be mocked. A man reaps what he sows." **Galatians 6:7 (NIV)**

The modern saying "What goes around, comes around," captures the essence of this Scripture. So if you and I want to have more stress-resistant lives, we need to sow the seeds of kindness so that we will receive an abundance of kindness in return.

> "Give generously for your gifts will return to you later. Divide your gifts among many for in the days ahead you yourself may need help."
> **Ecclesiastes 11:1 (LB)**

Among the ways that the Bible encourages us to be kind is by sharing our material possessions with those in need (1 John 3:17). We are also to visit the sick and those who are in prison. These are only a few of the ways that we can give kindness to others. You give when you smile at someone. You give when you share with others about your experiences with the Lord. Witnessing to others about Christ and letting His Spirit shine through your character and behavior are splendid ways of giving to others. Giving lifts our spirits and helps to reduce our feelings of helplessness about the conditions in our society.

There are so many social needs and problems to be solved. Find some constructive way to express the fact that you have said "Yes" to Christ and to His commandments that we love God and love people. Even if you can only help one person, you are choosing to align yourself with a cause higher than yourself.

Mother Teresa, who responded to God's call on her life by caring for and loving lepers, the dying and "the poorest of the poor," is a splendid example of someone who generously gave of herself. She said, "I am a little pencil in the hand of a writing God who is sending a love letter to the world." Those of us who passionately love God should resolve to let Him send a love letter to the world through us.

Use Wisdom With Your Kindness

Sometimes we increase the stresses in our lives and in the lives of others by being unwise in the ways in which we try to be loving and kind.

> *"For wisdom is better than rubies, And all the things one may desire cannot be compared with her."*
> **Proverbs 8:11 (NKJV)**

For example, when we actively love others, we not only try not to harm them, but we strive to protect them. To truly love them, we must use wisdom and self-control. For example, an overly protective parent harms his children as he excessively shields them. His worry and restrictions damage his children by depriving them of the opportunities to develop problem-solving, thinking, creative, social, and sometimes physical skills, such as riding a bike or driving a car. Overly protective parents harm their children by teaching them to fear the world and other people.

If you are being overly protective of someone you love, remember that God also loves that individual. Ask God to protect that person. Also pray for wisdom and self-control so that your protectiveness is appropriate.

As loving people, you and I also need to be wise and self-disciplined in order to avoid repeatedly protecting people from the consequences of addictions, poor money management and other self-destructive feelings and behaviors. For example:

Sean deeply loves his wife, Holly. Last year Sean discovered that Holly was an alcoholic. He pleaded with her to get help to stop drinking. Holly responded by dutifully going into an inpatient rehabilitation program. But Sean later learned that within two days after her release, Holly began drinking again.

He nagged her to attend AA meetings. She complied, but she continued to drink. The stress in the marriage grew as Sean felt his life going out of control in sync with Holly's. Desperate, Sean began attending a Christian 12-Step program for family and friends of substance abusers. There Sean learned that his efforts to protect Holly from the consequences of her alcoholism, by calling her employer to give excuses for Holly's absences, hiding her bottles of alcohol, etc., were not protecting her from harm

*after all. Sean learned that, on the contrary, he was actually
enabling her to harm herself.*

*With the support of the 12-Step group, Sean was able
to give Holly an ultimatum to give up drinking or their
marriage. In spite of her promises, Holly continued to
drink. Sean separated from her. That shocked Holly. It also
motivated her to begin to take responsibility for her
addiction. They have been separated for nine months. Holly
actively participates in a 12-Step program for Christians
and has not had a drink for six months.*

Although they are still separated, Holly and Sean are
seeing a marriage counselor who understands the dynamics
of alcoholism in family life. The level of stress in both of their
lives has decreased significantly because
Sean chose to use "tough love." That is,
Sean set limits on Holly and on his own
behavior. In the truest sense, by changing
his behavior and insisting that Holly
change hers, Sean was actively protecting
her and their relationship from harm. As a
result, Sean's love for Holly, for himself,
and for God has grown stronger.

*"Rebuke a wise
man, and he will
love you. Give
instruction to a
wise man and he
will be still wiser."*
Proverbs 9:8-9 (NKJV)

Live Peacefully With Others

To increase our resistance to the ravages of stress, each of us
should *"make every effort to live in peace with all men and to be
holy..."* **Hebrews 12:14** .

To live peaceably with others, we must make every
effort to show sensitivity and respect in our interactions with
them.

When we speak to or treat others with disrespect, our relationships with them deteriorate. We all know that conflicted interpersonal relationships can be major stressors. We help to avoid such distress when we make it a habit to be courteous and respectful to others. When we do this, even when we are angry, we reveal spiritual maturity and self-discipline (James 1:26).

"Let all...evil speaking be put away from you."

Ephesians 4:31 (NKJV)

However, in spite of our best efforts, there will be times when our relationships with others will have conflicts. When that happens we must try to resolve the conflicts quickly (Matthew 5:25). Christ taught that if someone has something against you, do not ignore it. As Christians, we must not shrug and say, "That's his or her problem, not mine." In Christ's perspective, the problem is also ours. He taught that we are to go to that person and try to work things out, i.e., be reconciled (Matthew 5:23-24). Whether or not the person accepts our efforts at reconciliation, we obey God when we try.

"Therefore if you bring your gift to the altar, and there remember that your brother has something against you, leave your gift there before the altar and go your way. First be reconciled to your brother, and then come and offer your gift."

Matthew 5:23-24 (NKJV)

In some cases, we should seek professional help for relationship problems that continue, in spite of our efforts to resolve them. We might also seek help for developing problems that seem to be getting worse. Don't wait until the problems become unmanageable or the relationship is beyond repair. Be a good steward of your relationships.

Be Patient

In our fast paced society, we are easily seduced into believing that things should happen fast. We want, "fast, fast, fast relief" of anything that distresses us. When we yield to our cultural teachings, we become impatient, especially with people. Our impatience stresses us and our relationships.

When, for instance, others don't change as fast as we want them to or in ways that we desire, some of us become tempted to throw away the relationship, just as we tend to throw away old clothes or appliances that still work, but are not the latest models. For example:

> *"But the fruit of the Spirit is love, joy, peace, longsuffering, kindness, goodness, faithfulness, gentleness, self-control."*
> **Galatians 5:22-23 (NKJV)**

> *Zelda has been married for a year and a half. "I love my husband," Zelda asserted. "But I'm tired of him messing up when it comes to paying the bills on time. I'm also not happy with our sex life. He just doesn't know how to please me sexually. If he doesn't straighten up soon," she said, "I'm outta here. I'm getting a divorce."*

The marriage is deteriorating under the weight of her, and sometimes his, impatient demands. To reduce their stress and to increase the likelihood of having a long-lasting and satisfying relationship, each of them must ask God to help him or her to be patient and long-suffering, i.e., willing to learn to tolerate each other's imperfections. They need to patiently work on improving their relationship. In some cases, such a couple should also seek the help of a Christian marriage counselor who can help them to develop the patience that is so crucial to a truly loving relationship.

126

Choose Friends Who Also Love God

As helpful as having a support system is to preventing, reducing, or managing stress, we must, nevertheless, use wisdom in choosing the people who will make up our support systems. In order to minimize your stress, try to avoid associating with negative thinking people. Although an overly optimistic person who sees life through "rose colored lenses" can be irritating, don't be duped into thinking that a pessimist is a realist. Negative thinking people will contribute to your depression, anxiety and sense of helplessness. The Bible condemns cynics, gossipers, rebels, and ungodly people (Romans 1:28-31). Such people should not be our companions.

> *"He who walks with the wise grows wise,but a companion of fools suffers harm."*
> **Proverbs 13:20 (NIV)**

Make friends with people who passionately love the Lord and affirm His life-style. When we fellowship with other lovers of God, our faith and hope are strengthened.

> *"And let us consider how we may spur one another on toward love and good deeds. Let us not give up meeting together...but let us encourage one another...."*
> **Hebrews 10:24-25 (NIV)**

What if it Is Hard for You to Love Others?

If you find it difficult to lovingly interact with people, because you are:

- ❖ highly distrustful of people,
- ❖ painfully shy,

127

❖ unable to make and/or keep friends, or are

❖ repeatedly drawn to destructive relationships

you should seek professional help. Positive, loving relationships with others are intrinsic to God's plan for His people. None of us thrive in isolation or alienation from others. Even if it appears, in the short term, that your stress is increased whenever you try to mend broken relationships, you will find that, in the long term, you will experience the blessings that God intends for those who are part of His love connection.

Find a trained Christian counselor who loves the Lord, people and him or herself. Let that person help you to overcome the emotional and mental obstacles to your full participation in God's stress management plan.

REMEMBER

1. You need good relationships with others to better avoid, reduce or manage stress.

2. Loving others increases the likelihood that you can have an effective support system.

3. If you truly love God, you will love other people as yourself.

In the process of relating with others, some of them may hurt or offend us. That can be very stressful. Let us see how God wants us to handle these experiences.

Principle 9
BE A FAST FORGIVER

"Judge not, and you shall not be judged. Condemn not, and you shall not be condemned. Forgive and you will be forgiven."

Luke 6:37 (RSV)

I am convinced that harboring grudges and refusing to forgive people are major causes of stress in many people's lives. Our passionate love of God compels us to seek to have a right relationship with Him. He requires not only that we seek His forgiveness when we offend Him, but that we forgive other people when they offend us.

> *"If you forgive others the wrongs they have done to you, your Father in heaven will also forgive you. But if you do not forgive others then your Father will not forgive the wrongs you have done."*
>
> **Matthew 5:14-15 (NIV)**

This is the great forgiveness equation. Since it is so vital to the relationships that we have with God, other people, and ourselves, you and I must earnestly develop forgiving attitudes. Years ago, someone asked Ruth Bell Graham, the wife of the great evangelist, Billy Graham, what was the secret of a happy marriage. She reportedly answered, "Be a fast forgiver."

In my own life and in the lives of the many people I have counseled, I see the wisdom of Mrs. Graham's advice. I believe that not only is being a fast forgiver a secret of a happy marriage, but is one of the secrets of decreasing stress in any relationship. Scientific studies have found that people who harbor anger, bitterness, and resentment have a higher risk of developing a range of physical, mental, and social problems, such as arthritis, cancer, high blood pressure, depression, anxiety and poor interpersonal relationships.

"And whenever you stand praying, if you have anything against anyone, forgive him, that your Father in heaven may also forgive you your trespasses. But if you do not forgive, neither will your Father in heaven forgive your trespasses."

Mark 11:25 (NKJV)

Jesus taught that when someone did wrong to us that we should forgive that person *"seventy times seven"* (Matthew 18: 21-35), I understand this to mean that there is no real limit to the number of times that we are to forgive other people. I thought that this teaching was primarily for the benefit of the person who had committed the offense. I now believe that this important teaching is for the benefit of both parties. When we forgive, reconciliation is possible. In fact, without forgiveness, true reconciliation is impossible. Unforgiveness has an eroding effect on both people. But it is most grievous for the person who withholds forgiveness. For instance:

> *Ted still gets furious each time he thinks about his father. His father spent a lot of time away from the family when Ted was growing up. Much of that time he was having affairs with other women. Ted's blood pressure becomes elevated as he remembers the pain and embarrassment his*

mother felt about his father's behavior. The bitterness Ted feels about his father's neglect of him has affected Ted so that he has not been able to establish with his own son the kind of warm relationship he so wanted to have with his dad. Sometimes, Ted spends hours feeling sorry for the childhood he never had. When he does this, his wife and children experience him as unpleasant to be around. Ted's father has been dead for eight years. Ted is trapped in his own unforgiveness.

Some of the wrongs that are done to us are more easily forgiven than are others. For example:

Erika forgave her father for being overly restrictive of her and her siblings. She came to understand that this was his way of trying to keep them from getting into trouble. However, it took over twenty years for her to even consider forgiving him for shooting and killing her mother in a fit of rage.

Erika's inability to forgive her father contaminated her relationships with all of the men in her life. For years, she was high strung, easily angered, suspicious, and depressed. She only began to heal when she asked God to help her to forgive her father.

When you and I encounter offenses hard to forgive, we must pray and ask the Lord to help us. Jesus said, "*Ask and you shall receive*" (Matthew 7:7). Because we will be asking God to help us to do something He requires us to do, we are assured of His help.

Forgiveness is often a process. Full forgiveness for some offenses requires more than making a decision to "let bygones be bygone." Complete forgiveness of some offenses may take time to complete. Jesus taught us specific steps of the process of forgiveness. He said:

"Love your enemies, do good to those who hate you, bless those who curse you, pray for those who mistreat you."

Luke 6:27 (NIV)

This prescription for forgiveness is radically different from what we would do on our own. We need to be empowered by our passionate love relationships with God to obtain the power to do this. Christ said that if we do follow these specific steps,

"Then your reward will be great, and you will be sons (and daughters) of the most High because He is kind to the ungrateful and wicked. Be merciful, just as your Father is merciful."

Luke 6:35-36 (NIV)

This does not mean that if someone continually wrongs you that you should continue to allow him or her to do so — unless you are certain that this is God's will for you in your specific circumstances. It may be important that we confront the offenders about their behaviors. It may mean that we remove ourselves from situations in which we are constantly exploited or abused. For example, when I was a speaker at a women's retreat, one of the women wrote me the following letter. She wanted me to read it to the entire group and give my response. The letter read:

Dear Dr Mendes;

I have been in counseling for several years with my husband. We still have many marital problems. The relationship has been verbally, physically, and emotionally

abusive. I am mentally and physically drained. I have talked to the church counselors numerous times. I know God does not believe in divorce. I'm constantly praying. Do I stay in this abusive situation? How can a Christian woman continue to have faith in this environment?

Sincerely,

K.T.

I was glad to share my answer to her question before the hundreds of women who were at the retreat. I suspected that K.T. was not the only one having that problem. I told the women that I did not believe that our loving God intended for any of us to keep ourselves in any relationship in which we are continually abused physically and emotionally. We all know that spousal abuse has caused the deaths of many women. It is inconceivable that this would be in God's will for wives and husbands. I told K.T. that even if she did not want to divorce her husband, she was free to leave him. She still is under the Biblical obligation to forgive her husband, but she did not have to continue to live with him to prove her forgiveness.

All of us must remember that unforgiveness is an acid that eats away one's peace of mind. Keeping a record of the wrongs others have done condemns you and me to mentally reliving the offenses. As you and I repeatedly review past hurts, we renew our

"Husbands, love your wives just as Christ also loved the Church and gave Himself for her.... So husbands ought to love their own wives as their own bodies; he who loves his wife loves himself."

Ephesians 5:25, 28 (NKJV)

"See then that you walk circumspectly, not as fools but as wise. Therefore do not be unwise, but understand what the will of the Lord is."

Ephesians 5:25, 28 (NKJV)

133

anger and feelings of victimization. Consequently, our stress levels increase. On the other hand, we become more stress-resistant when we quickly forgive others and refuse to hold grudges.

If someone whom we trusted betrays us, we must forgive that individual. However, the decision about how soon, if ever, we should again trust that person requires that we use wisdom. As James 1:5 tells us, we should ask God for the wisdom we need, and He will give it to us.

Since any degree of unforgiveness can play such a pivotal role in causing stress to ravage your health and well being, take time now to prayerfully consider how fast a forgiver you are.

* Make a list of people for whom you feel resentment, grudges, and other forms of unforgiveness-however faint the feelings.

* Add to the list any one whom you think you have forgiven, but with whom you are annoyed, angry or critical. Often people don't *feel* their unforgiveness because they have suppressed it into their unconscious. Nevertheless, the unforgiveness reveals itself in anger or criticism directed at the offender or someone associated with the offender.

* Prayerfully review the list and decide to forgive these people.

* Be specific about the offenses for which you are forgiving them. You may have to do this more than once. Each time you find yourself

> *"Therefore be imitators of God as dear children. And walk in love, as Christ also has loved us and given Himself for us...."*
>
> **Ephesians 5:1-2**

dwelling on the pain, humiliation, or other strong emotions evoked by the offense, remind yourself that you have released your unforgiveness. The goal is not to forget the offense. God does not ask you to tamper with your memory. Rather, the goal is to experience God's peace, whenever you do remember the offense.

❖ Whenever you find it especially hard to forgive someone, pray for that person. Pray for God to bless and heal that individual. Pray that God will flood your heart with His love so that you can obey Him by forgiving.

❖ If it is possible, "do good" to that hard-to-forgive person (Luke 6:27). Sometimes, the only way that this is possible is to ask God to do good things for that offender. This may be the wisest way to do good when it is dangerous to you or to others for you to personally interact with that individual.

❖ Sometimes, the offense and the circumstances surrounding it are so painful that you need to talk about it with someone. Talk to a mature Christian whom you trust. Make sure your confidant loves God, is compassionate, wise, discreet, and non-judgmental. Have that person pray for you and for the offender.

"I, therefore,…the prisoner of the Lord, beseech you to walk worthy of the calling with which you were called, with all lowliness and gentleness, with long suffering, bearing with one another in love, endeavoring to keep the unity of the Spirit in the bond of peace."

Ephesians 4:1-3 (NKJV)

135

REMEMBER

Resolve to become a fast forgiver.

1. Don't be easily angered or hold grudges.

2. Stop holding personal "pity parties" at which you enjoy the misery of feeling like a victim.

3. Follow Christ's prescriptions for dealing with those who offend you

4. Experience the joy of God's forgiveness of your offenses against Him as you forgive those who offend you.

Principle 10
STAY CONNECTED

"As the Father loved me,
I also have loved you; abide in My love."
John 15:9

Within a relatively short time, the Apostle Paul was:

❖ thrown in jail merely because he said what he believed about God.

❖ a victim of police brutality.

❖ assaulted by an angry mob.

He often:

❖ did not have enough food.

❖ was cold, because he did not have warm clothing.

❖ had trouble sleeping.

❖ worried about the people he loved.

(2 Corinthians 11:23-28)

Yet, Paul who described himself as "weak" (2 Corinthians 11:30, 12:5) showed no signs of "burn out." Neither did he "freak out" or give any indications that these horrendous stressors got him down. What was his secret?

His "secret" was his love connection to God through Christ.

"...I have learned to be content whatever the circumstances. I know what it is to be in need, and I know what it is to have plenty. I have learned the secret of being content in any and every situation, whether well fed or hungry, whether living in plenty or in want. I can do all things through Christ who strengthens me."

Philippians 4:11-13 (NIV)

Paul trusted that he could draw the strength he needed from God. With his connection to Him, Paul was confident that he could deal with anything life sent his way.

The prophet Isaiah also knew the strength which comes from a love connection to God and His power. Isaiah said,

"The Lord is the everlasting God...He gives strength to the weary and increases the power of the weak...those who hope in the Lord will renew their strength. They will soar on wings like eagles. They will run and not grow weary. They will walk and not be faint...."

Isaiah 40:28-29 (NIV)

The strengthening power that God gave to Paul and to Isaiah is available to us today. For example, Dr Leona Byas said:

"Given what I went through, I should be in a mental hospital.

"The reason that I'm not," she continued, "is that God sustained me."

"Unless the Lord had been my help, My soul would soon have settled in silence. If I say 'My foot slips,' Your mercy, O Lord, will hold me up. In the multitude of my anxieties within me. Your comforts delight my soul."

Psalm 94:17-19 (NKJV)

Dr. Byas told the congregation at the Crystal Cathedral in Garden Grove, California, and the millions of viewers around the world who watched that televised service, about the power of God in her life. Her son, Len Byas, a promising young professional basketball player, suddenly died a drug-related death. Her intense grief had barely subsided when another son was murdered.

"Finally, my brethren, be strong in the Lord and in the power of His might."

Ephesians 6:10 (NKJV)

"God gave me the strength to rise above the utter devastation I felt at losing my two young sons, my babies," she declared.

Undoubtedly, other viewers around the world were as transfixed as I was by this woman who, through her love relationship with God, had turned those painful losses into an inspiring testimonial about God's sustaining power.

You and I need God to empower us to cope with whatever life brings us. Unfortunately, some of us close ourselves off from this power. Some of us allow our pride to get in the way of our experiencing the vitality God wants to give to us. Many of us find it embarrassing to ask for help, even God's help. We'd rather do it ourselves. We feel vulnerable and childlike when we ask for help. We are much more comfortable relying upon our own intelligence, will power, money, and other resources, which we believe are under our control. Such pride blinds us to the reality that apart from God, we can do nothing.

Some of us are like Farmer Banks. The story goes that Farmer Banks proudly strolled out of the hardware store, delighted with the brand-new chain saw he had just bought.

It was guaranteed to cut ten big oak trees an hour. Twenty-four hours later, an obviously frustrated Banks was back at the store complaining that the saw would never cut ten trees an hour. "This saw only cut three trees all day long!" he bellowed. Puzzled, the storeowner stepped outside with the saw. He gave the cord a rip, firing up the steel-toothed beast. Farmer Banks was so startled by the deafening roar of the saw that he stumbled backwards. "What's that noise?" he shrieked.

"Beware lest anyone cheat you through philosophy and empty deceit, according to the tradition of men, according to the basic principles of the world, and not according to Christ."

Colossians 2:8

Farmer Bank's error in trying to cut down trees without starting up the chain saw is very much like the foolishness of our trying to live life on our own strength. We inflict upon ourselves untold stresses, when we try to make our lives work on our own terms. God's power becomes available to us only when we begin to love Him passionately and trust Him for the stress-resistant life we cannot live apart from Him.

"You shall love the Lord your God with all your heart, with all your soul, and with all your mind. This is the first and great commandment. And the second is like it: You shall love your neighbor as yourself."

Matthew 22:37-39

RESOURCES

Daily Devotionals

Bible Pathway Ministries
P.O. Box 20123
Murfreesboro, Tennessee 37129-0123
Phone: 615-896-4243
Fax: 615-893-1744
E-mail: mail@biblepathway.org
Credit Card Orders only: 1-800-598-7884

Thru the Bible in One Year Reading 15 minutes a day. Scriptures taken from the King James Version.

Radio Bible Class Ministries
U.S.A: P.O. Box 2222, Grand Rapids, Michigan 49501-2222
Canada: Box 1622, Windsor, Ontario N9A 6Z7
RBC Web site: www.rbc.net

Our Daily Bread, a devotional with Daily Scriptures and a guide to reading the Bible in One Year.

For more in-depth Bible study, RBC offers online general courses on the Old and New Testaments, plus courses about specific books of the Bible. Visit www.ChristianCourses.com to find out more,

Mental Health Services

Focus on the Family
8605 Explorer Drive
Colorado Spring, Colorado 80995

Through radio broadcasts, books, tapes, videos, CDs and seminars Focus on the Family's mission is to cooperate with the Holy Spirit in disseminating the Gospel of Jesus Christ to as many people as possible and specifically to accomplish that objective by helping to preserve traditional values and the institution of the family.

Mendes Consultation Services
3660 Wilshire Blvd., Suite 907
Los Angeles, California 90010
Phone: 213-388-6668
Fax: 310-798-4164
E-mail: hmendeslov@aol.com

MCS utilizes Biblical principles, and scientific theories and techniques that are compatible with Scriptures to help people solve personal, marital, family and work-related problems. Services include counseling, key note speeches, seminars, consulting, books and tapes.

Overcomers Outreach
P.O. Box 2208
Oakhurst, California 93644 USA
Phone: 1 (88) 310-3001
E-mail: info@overcomersoutreach.org

In CANADA: Overcomers Canada 165
E-mail: overcomer@mb.imag.net

GERMANY: http://.endlich-leben.net/dox/overcomers.htm

UNITED KINGDOM: E-mail: Mel@luke79.freeserve.co.uk or call Ronnie B. at 020 8773-1594

Overcomers Outreach is a ministry that was born out of a deep need of a support system for individuals and families within evangelical Christian churches. Overcomers Outreach support groups use the Bible and the 12 steps of Alcoholics Anonymous to minister to individuals who are affected by alcohol, mind altering drugs, sexual addiction, gambling, food and other compulsive behaviors or dependencies. Family members are welcome at meetings.

Pine Rest Christian Mental Health Services
300 68th Street SE
P. O. Box 165, Grand Rapids, Michigan 49501
Phone: 616-455-9200 or 455-5000
Des Moines, Iowa Clinic: 515-334-9911

Pine Rest CMHS is called to express the healing ministry of Jesus Christ by providing behavioral health services with professional excellence, Christian integrity and compassion.

About the Author

Dr. Helen A. Mendes is president of Mendes Consultation Services of Los Angeles. She has over 40 years experience in helping people solve stressful personal, marital, family and work-related problems. Although Dr. Mendes finds value in a variety of approaches to stress management, she finds none equals the power of Biblical principles for helping people to avoid, reduce or better manage stress.

Dr. Mendes earned her master degree in social work at Columbia University and her doctorate at UCLA. She studied theology at Fuller Theological seminary. For eleven years, she was a professor of social work at the University of Southern California where she taught master and Ph.D students. She was also on the faculties of UCLA, Hunter College School of Social Work and the Albert Einstein College of Medicine of Yeshiva University. She is a member of the Academy of Social Workers, a Diplomat in Clinical Social Work and is a licensed Clinical Social Worker in the state of California. Dr. Mendes teaches social work at Pepperdine University in Malibu, California.

She is a popular guest speaker and gives workshops and seminars for professional and lay audiences. She consults with and trains executive and line staff at corporate, non-profit and military organizations on improving human relationships in the workplace.

144

Dr. Mendes is the author of *The African Heritage Cookbook*, a history-recipe book published by McMillan & Co. and author of numerous articles, she has been quoted in the *Los Angeles Times*, *Christian Science Monitor*, *San Francisco Chronicle*, *Essence Magazine*, *Redbook Magazine* and *Human Behavior Magazine*. She has also been a guest on radio and television including: KCBS, KNBC, KACE, KJLH and KZLA.

Dr. Helen Mendes is a recipeint of UCLA's Distinguished Scholarship Award, Zeta Phi Beta Sorority Woman of the Year Award in Education, Award of Merit for Outstanding Service to USC School of Social Work and a Woman of Religious Achievement Award. She is listed in Who's Who Among Black Americans, Who's Who Among American Women, World's Who's Who of Women and the Out- standing People of the 20th Century.

Dr. Mendes is a devout Christian who integrates a Christian Worldview in her psychotherapy practice. Dr. Mendes says, "My goal is to help people grow in their faith in God and their commitments to Him. I want to help people to learn first-hand how wonderfully effective Biblical principles are for enabling people to deal victoriously with the inevitable problems of life."

HOW YOU CAN HELP DR. MENDES HELP OTHERS

It will take the efforts of many people for the important messages contained in *God's Stress Management Plan* to reach millions of people who are needlessly suffering from harmful stress.

Think about and write in how this message has helped you, that in turn will help others.

We would very much like to hear from you. Please send your comments about the book to us in care of the address below. Thank you.

Vicstone Publishing Company
3660 Wilshire Blvd. Suite 907
Los Angeles, California 90010
E-Mail: vicstone.publishing@verizon.net

Dr. Mendes is available for keynote speeches, seminars and retreats. She may be contacted at:

(213) 388-6668 or   **E-Mail: hmendeslov@aol.com**

God's Stress Management Plan   (ISBN: 0-9744482-0-6) is $19.95 for softbound edition, plus $4.00 shipping for first copy ($1.50 each additional copy) and sales tax for California orders.